Improving Standards-Based Learning

Improving Standards-Based Learning

*A **Process Guide** for Educational Leaders*

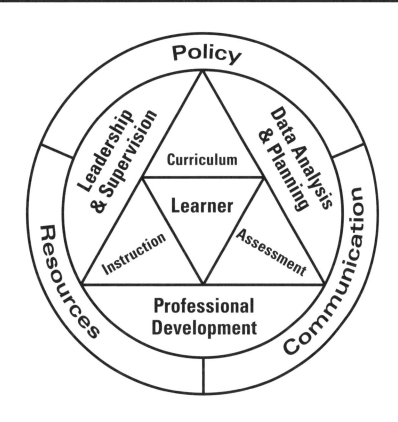

Judy F. Carr   Doug Harris

CORWIN
A SAGE Company

310220476

8-6-09

Some material in this book appeared in Carr, J. & Harris, D. (1993) Getting it together: A process workbook for K–12 curriculum, instruction, and assessment. Boston: Allyn and Bacon.

For information:

Corwin
A SAGE Company
2455 Teller Road
Thousand Oaks, California 91320
(800) 233-9936
Fax: (800) 417-2466
www.corwinpress.com

SAGE India Pvt. Ltd.
B 1/I 1 Mohan Cooperative
    Industrial Area
Mathura Road, New Delhi 110 044
India

SAGE Ltd.
1 Oliver's Yard
55 City Road
London EC1Y 1SP
United Kingdom

SAGE Asia-Pacific Pte. Ltd.
33 Pekin Street #02-01
Far East Square
Singapore 048763

Printed in the United States of America

Library of Congress Cataloging-in-Publication Data

Carr, Judy F.
Improving standards-based learning : a process guide for educational leaders/Judy F. Carr and Doug Harris.
    p. cm.
Includes bibliographical references and index.
ISBN 978-1-4129-6569-9 (cloth)
ISBN 978-1-4129-6570-5 (pbk.)

    1. School improvement programs—United States. 2. Education—Standards—United States. 3. Curriculum planning—United States. I. Harris, Douglas E. II. Title.

LB2822.82.C365 2009
371.2'07—dc22   2009003666

This book is printed on acid-free paper.

09   10   11   12   13   10   9   8   7   6   5   4   3   2   1

Acquisitions Editor:	Debra Stollenwerk
Editorial Assistant:	Julie McNall
Production Editor:	Amy Schroller
Copy Editor:	Claire Larson
Typesetter:	C&M Digitals (P) Ltd.
Proofreader:	Charlotte Waisner
Indexer:	Sylvia Coates
Cover Designer:	Dan Irwin
Graphic Designer:	Brian Bello

Contents

List of Worksheets

CHAPTER 3. PREPARING FOR COMMITTEE MEETINGS
44

CHAPTER 4. GROUP DYNAMICS: A GUIDE FOR THE COMMITTEE CHAIR
55

CHAPTER 5. DEVELOPING THE K–12 CURRICULUM GUIDELINES
69

CHAPTER 6. PUBLISHING AND CELEBRATING THE DOCUMENT 96

CHAPTER 7. DEVELOPMENT OF COMMON ASSESSMENTS: A DESIGN OVERVIEW 111

CHAPTER 8. PLANNING FOR IMPLEMENTATION 122

CHAPTER 9. THREE STRATEGIES TO SUPPORT IMPLEMENTATION   137

CHAPTER 10. CURRICULUM-BASED PROGRAM EVALUATION   152

Preface

One hot June day many years ago, we met briefly at 7:30 in the morning to exchange materials before heading off for separate consulting jobs in school districts 150 miles apart. As we talked, we discovered we had each been hired to do essentially the same thing: help administrators and teachers design models and processes to improve curriculum in their districts. The questions posed to us in both places were remarkably similar: How is curriculum put together? What should be included? Who should be involved? How long will it take? How should we go about it?

These questions were not unlike those asked of us in many other school districts that did not have a curriculum generalist on staff—and many do not. For several years, while both employed by school districts, we had received far more requests to consult on curriculum projects than either of us could possibly accommodate. More and more frequently, we found ourselves sending off materials we had developed in our own work to aid those whose requests for direct assistance we were forced to refuse. Feedback we received indicated that the materials we provided served very well in our absence.

Over time, we had grown increasingly concerned about the questions we were rarely asked: What should be considered and acted upon in implementing the curriculum? How is curriculum evaluated? In far too many districts, energy seemed to be focused only on completing the written curriculum guide, rather than on the quality of the experience and learning of students. If the time spent on curriculum development is ultimately to be valued by teachers and to benefit students, it must be followed by sufficient support in the form of materials, planning time, and professional development required to implement the curriculum, as well as by systematic attention to results. Any one of these components alone is unlikely to result in substantive improvement of learning and teaching.

That brief early-morning conversation was the starting point for this book, designed to guide educators throughout the curriculum process. Since that time, states across the nation have adopted standards for student learning and have implemented programs of high-stakes testing based on those standards and their associated performance indicators and grade-level expectations. Technology applications in schools and districts have grown exponentially. Schools and districts continue to struggle with designing, implementing, and evaluating systems of standards-based curriculum. This book reflects these realities and includes material on the design of common assessments, while at the same time providing a simple, straightforward process schools and districts can use to guide them through the process of developing curriculum systems.

SPECIAL FEATURES OF THIS BOOK

This book is a toolkit of essential resources to support development, implementation, and evaluation of high quality curriculum in schools and districts and includes

- Guidelines to lead the reader through the process
- Examples from schools and districts

- Worksheets to guide the processes described in the text
- Graphics that illustrate key points,
- Strategies that have been proven to work,
- Vignettes to illustrate key content, and
- Questions to promote reflection.

GUIDING QUESTIONS

Many questions must be answered in designing a curriculum development, implementation, and evaluation cycle, as shown in Figure P.1.

These questions establish the framework for this book, and ways and means to approach answering them are detailed in the chapters that follow. The comprehensive process that is provided can be tailored to meet the needs of particular schools and districts. Those who are more experienced will likely be able to combine steps or skip steps altogether. For example, in districts in which a vision statement has recently been adopted, there is no need to create another one. Those just beginning curriculum work will find it helpful to review the entire book and then work through it chapter by chapter.

Figure P.1 Considerations in the Development of a Districtwide Curriculum Process

What is the district's vision for standards and student learning?
What is the timeline for curriculum development, implementation, and evaluation?

Development

Before:

- How will information from the current program evaluation be used?
- What resources are needed?

  ○ How much time will it take?
  ○ When will meetings take place?
  ○ How much will it cost?
  ○ What materials are required?
  ○ What standards and performance indicators will be incorporated?
  ○ What training do committee members need?
  ○ What sources of expertise are available (consultants, access to current educational literature, staff members, sample curriculum documents from other districts, etc.)?
  ○ Is sufficient clerical support available?

- What will be the size and composition of committees (representation, selection vs. appointment, etc.)?
- Who will serve as chairperson?

During:

- How will the committee solicit and receive input and feedback?
- At what points in the process will this be done?
- How will communication with teachers, administrators, and the community take place?
- What are the ground rules for committee meetings?
- How will curriculum documents be approved?
- What is the basis for decision making?
- What issues and concerns may arise during the development process?

(Continued)

Figure P.1 (Continued)

After:

- What besides scope and sequence will the curriculum guidelines contain?
  - ○ Purpose Statement?
  - ○ Goals?
  - ○ Materials and Resources?
  - ○ Instructional Guidelines?
  - ○ Needs and Recommendations?
  - ○ Program Evaluation Statement?
  - ○ Appendices?
  - ○ Glossary?
  - ○ Bibliography?
  - ○ Timelines?

Implementation

Before:

- How will the curriculum be phased in?
  - ○ What training and support do teachers and administrators require or desire?
  - ○ How much money will it cost?
  - ○ How much time will it take?
  - ○ What materials are required?
- How will all teachers and administrators be provided with the opportunity to become familiar with the contents of the curriculum document?
- How will community members become familiar with the curriculum?
- Who is responsible for what?

During:

- Do student/teacher interactions (learning experiences provided, materials and instructional strategies used) match the intent and specifications of the instructional guidelines?
- How are students provided with opportunities to master the objectives and attain the goals of the curriculum?
- How is the learning of individual students assessed and evaluated?
- What common assessments are needed?
- How is the curriculum reflected in day-to-day decision making and communication?
  - ○ Budget?
  - ○ Staff development?
  - ○ Teacher evaluation?

After:

- Do student learning outcomes match the goals and objectives of the curriculum?

Evaluation

Before:

- What questions need to be answered through program evaluation? (Note: These need to be based directly on the curriculum guidelines.)
- What methods of assessment are best suited to the questions?
- What assessment tools are best suited to answer the assessment questions?
- What resources are needed?
  - ○ Time?
  - ○ Money?
  - ○ Expertise?
- Who is responsible for what?

During:

- How will data be collected? By whom?
- How will the data be analyzed? By whom?

After:

- Who will write the evaluation report?
- What will the report contain?
- How will the results be used?
- How will the results be communicated? To whom?

Acknowledgments

We are grateful to the many colleagues in the school districts and educational organizations listed below from whom we have learned so much about standards-based curriculum, instruction, and assessment.

The Enlarged City School District of Middletown (New York)

Elmira City School District (New York)

Oswego City School District (New York)

Washington Central School District (Vermont)

Addison Northeast School District (Vermont)

Franklin Northeast Supervisory Union (Vermont)

South Burlington School District (Vermont)

Franklin Northwest Supervisory Union (Vermont)

Essex Town School District (Vermont)

Sarasota County School Board (Florida)

Manatee County School Board (Florida)

Trinity College of Vermont

The University of South Florida at Sarasota–Manatee

The University of Vermont

The Vermont Department of Education

The Vermont Institutes

Many thanks to Debra Stollenwerk and Julie McNall at Corwin whose vision, skill, and attention to details enhanced the quality of this publication.

About the Authors

Judy F. Carr, EdD, and Doug Harris, PhD, are codirectors of the Center for Curriculum Renewal (www.curriculumrenewal.com), working as consultants, leadership coaches, facilitators, professional development specialists, workshop presenters, and program evaluators with educators and policymakers throughout the United States, Canada, and the Caribbean. They are coauthors of the following books:

- *How to Use Standards in the Classroom* (Association for Supervision and Curriculum Development, 1998)
- *Succeeding With Standards: Linking Curriculum, Assessment, and Action Planning* (Association for Supervision and Curriculum Development, 2001)
- *Creating Dynamic Schools Through Mentoring, Coaching, and Collaboration* (Association for Supervision and Curriculum Development, 2005)

Judy Carr is also a scholar in residence in the College of Education at the University of South Florida at Sarasota–Manatee, teaching half-time in the educational leadership program with a focus on school curriculum improvement, administrative analysis and change, and theoretical and historical aspects of curriculum and leadership. In 1995, she received the Second Annual Vermont ASCD Outstanding Education Leadership Award.

Additional books coauthored or coedited by Judy Carr are

- *Integrated Studies in the Middle Grades: Dancing Through Walls* (Teachers College Press, 1992)
- *Living and Learning in the Middle Grades: The Dance Continues: A Festschrift for Chris Stevenson* (National Middle School Association, 2001)
- *Teaching and Leading From the Inside Out* (Corwin, 2007)

Doug Harris is also executive director of the Vermont Institutes, providing professional development and technical assistance in the areas of mathematics, technology, research, and evaluation. He has significant experience in developing standards-based curriculum, instruction, and assessment, as well as in evaluating educational programs and initiatives. Harris served the public schools as a teacher, principal, assistant superintendent, and superintendent. He has directed major federally funded projects for the National Gardening Association, the Vermont Institute for Science, Math, and Technology, and the Vermont Institutes. He is a former member of Association for Supervision and Curriculum Development's Executive Council, a founding member of the ASCD Assessment Consortium, a member of the Board of the International Graduate Center, and a frequent contributor to Vermont and national policy initiatives.

1

Creating the Focus for Standards-Based Learning

Standards provide the focus for the design, implementation, and evaluation of high quality programs and practices for student learning. Many decisions are involved in the development of these processes, and these should be based on the district's and schools' vision for standards-based learning, awareness of state and federal mandates, synthesis of related educational research literature and recommendations of professional organizations, and an analysis of the existing curriculum in the district.

DESIGNING A MODEL FOR STANDARDS-BASED LEARNING

Before we clarified our own conceptual model for standards-based learning, we had been working as consultants to school districts for several years, supporting their efforts to implement standards. Initially this work entailed working with representative committees to facilitate their design of district and school curriculum guidelines based on standards, including scope and sequence documents, instructional parameters, criteria for classroom assessment, and so forth. As curriculum guidelines were completed, questions arose about the "how" of their implementation: *How can teachers use these new standards-based scope-and-sequence documents in the classroom? How do we align existing textbooks and other materials with the scope-and-sequence documents? How do we know if students are learning what is set forth in these documents?* This led to work with leadership teams in schools and districts and to the design of tools and processes to support the implementation and evaluation of standards-based learning.

One day we were working with a team of teachers on assignment in the Oswego City School District in New York when the superintendent of schools, Dr. Kenneth Eastwood, returned from presenting a session at a national conference. Afterward, he said, "A woman came up to me and commented that we were doing such good work in the district, but there was nothing on our Web site that made clear how all the pieces and parts connected one to the other."

A paper napkin was on the table where we were sitting, and we began to sketch out a graphic that captured our vision of the system of standards-based learning. Within two hours, the district's fine print shop had produced a poster of the design, which in one form is used on the district's Web site and in another has become the conceptual model we use in our work through the Center for Curriculum Renewal (www.curriculumrenewal.org) with schools and districts, as shown in Figure 1.1.

Figure 1.1 Standards-Based Learning

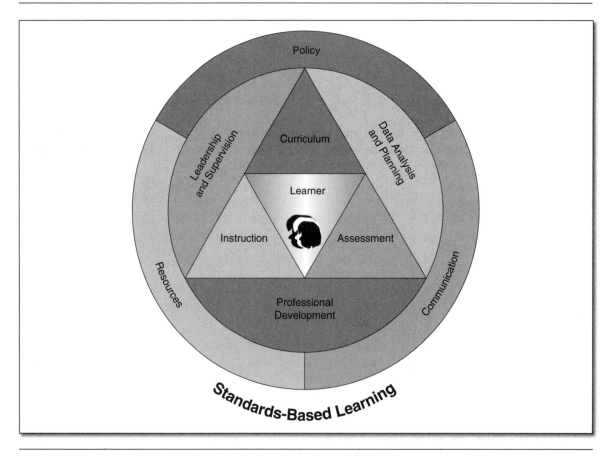

Source: Center for Curriculum Renewal (www.curriculumrenewal.com). Used with permission.

This model shows the learners at the center, representing the importance of addressing each learner's needs *and* strengths at the heart of the system of standards-based learning. The alignment, then, of curriculum, instruction, and assessment ties also to the identified strengths and needs of learners. Each district's and school's decisions about what standards, performance indicators, and grade-level expectations are taught and assessed at what grade level and in what time frame (e.g., quarter, month) become an important part of the curriculum triangle. Classroom assessments and common assessments need to actually assess the learning articulated in the curriculum documents (instead of merely assessing the quality of products or student comprehension of a story in a basal reader). Planning for instruction involves design of instructional strategies that can serve as building blocks from the student's current knowledge and skills to the desired learning identified in the curriculum.

The next ring in the model identifies the three components of the system designed to support teachers as they work with students in the classroom—data analysis and planning, professional development, and leadership and supervision. Resources, policies, and communication must also be aligned if standards-based learning is to be as effective and efficient as possible, leading ultimately to positive performance results for all students regardless of identified learning needs, socioeconomic status, race, gender, or culture.

The Elmira City School District and the Enlarged City School District of Middletown are two New York districts that have adapted the model to make it their own, as shown in Figure 1.2 and Figure 1.3.

Each of these districts has used the graphic for the model to organize resources for standards-based learning at their respective Web sites (http://www.middletowncityschools.org/SBL/SBLhome.htm and http://www.elmiracityschools.com/curriculumhome.cfm). We use the original conceptual model described above to organize links to resources at our own Web site, www.curriculumrenewal.com.

Does your district have a model for standards-based learning to show the relationships among the various essential components of your standards-based system? If so, how does it compare to model(s) shown above? Is there anything you would change? Add? Delete? If your school or district does not have a model for standards-based learning, consider designing one for your own school or the district as a whole.

DEVELOPING THE DISTRICT'S AND SCHOOLS' VISION FOR STANDARDS-BASED LEARNING

The district's or schools' vision for standards-based learning builds off the conceptual model and is a statement of beliefs about learning and a commitment to put those beliefs into action. This

Figure 1.2 Elmira City School District's Standards-Based Model

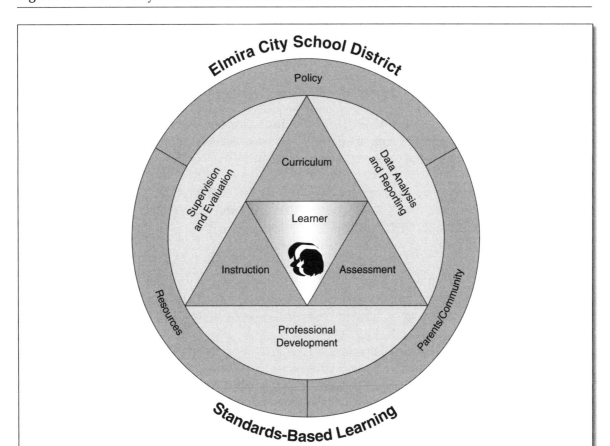

Source: Elmira City School District, Elmira, NY. Used with permission.

Figure 1.3 Enlarged City School District of Middletown's Standards-Based Model

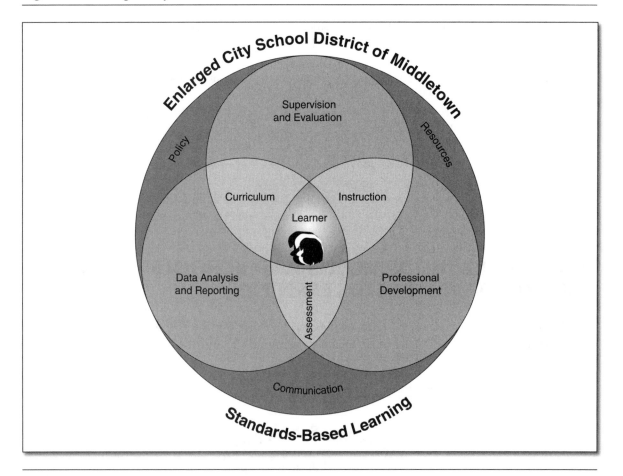

Source: Enlarged City School District of Middletown, NY. Used with permission.

document should guide all decision making in the district pertaining to curriculum development, implementation, and evaluation. Figure 1.4 provides an example of a comprehensive vision statement for standards-based learning developed some years ago by the Washington Central Supervisory Union in Vermont.

Washington Central's articulation of their vision is extensive, and it provided clear expectations and targets for schools across the district. The Franklin Northeast Supervisory Union began with the work Washington Central had done, and the district's administrative team decided they wanted a shorter, more compact articulation of their own vision, as shown in Figure 1.5.

If a school or district vision for standards-based learning already exists, it is important to evaluate its currency and its comprehensiveness. You may need to revise the statement to better reflect the current beliefs and commitment in the district. Use Worksheet 1.1, Evaluating Your Existing Vision Statement, to determine whether or not there is a need to revise your district philosophy or mission statement.

If your district has no vision statement, or if the existing vision statement does not directly address standards-based learning, it would be wise to begin creating one prior to beginning your process of designing a curriculum development, implementation, and evaluation cycle. One way to do this is to begin with the Washington Central Supervisory Union's Vision for Standards-Based Learning presented in Figure 1.4. One or more groups of administrators, teachers, parent and community members, or students can use Worksheet 1.2, Reflections on a District Vision for Student-Centered, Standards-Based Learning, to consider what works for your school's or district's vision statement, what doesn't work, and what needs to be changed. This input can then be used in drafting a next version for the consideration of members of the school community.

Some schools and districts prefer to start from scratch. Figure 1.6, Creating a Vision Statement, suggests a process to use in the design of a vision statement. Worksheets 1.3 through 1.7 are designed to help you accomplish this task.

Figure 1.4 Washington Central Supervisory Union's Vision for Standards-Based Learning

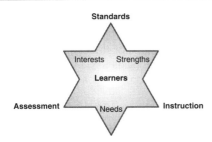

Excellence and Equity: ALL Kids Can!

WCSU Vision for Student-Centered, Standards-Based Education

The Washington Central Supervisory Union is a community of learners—adults and children working and learning together. We respond to the unique interests, needs, and strengths of each learner and to improving the learning of ALL students.

What We Mean By "All Students"

By "all students," we mean specifically (adapted from the National Council of Teachers of Mathematics, 1989):

- students who have been denied access in any way to educational opportunities, as well as those who have not;
- students who are female, as well as those who are male;
- students who are African-American, Hispanic, American Indian, or members of other minorities, as well as those who are part of the racial or ethnic majority;
- students who are socioeconomically disadvantaged, as well as those who are more advantaged; and
- students who have not been successful in school, as well as those who have been successful.

A very small percentage of Vermont students may not meet the standards adopted by WCSU because of the extreme severity of their disabilities. An example might be a high school student with a severe disability who functions at a preschool academic level. Accommodations for such students should be specifically addressed in their Individualized Educational Programs, within the spirit and context of what these standards intend.

WCSU Mission Statement: Our Commitment to Continuous Improvement

We value continuous improvement, building on the best of what exists to enhance the experience and performance of learners.

- WCSU ensures all students receive equitable, appropriate, and highest quality educational opportunities to maximize each child's unique academic, artistic, social, emotional, and physical development.
- WCSU has adopted the *Vermont Framework of Standards and Learning Opportunities* and determined what vital results standards and evidence and what fields-of-knowledge standards and evidence will be taught and assessed in which grade levels in all schools. Curriculum, instruction, and assessment will be aligned with these decisions and with Vermont's learning opportunities at all levels.
- WCSU establishes high instructional expectations for staff members to challenge all students to meet standards.
- WCSU provides professional development opportunities linked to standards and assessment and focused on improving student performance.
- WCSU provides economic and administrative efficiencies by utilizing the collective resources and expertise of the member schools.
- WCSU fosters collaborative partnerships among citizens, schools, families, and businesses to build a healthy community for our youth.
- WCSU prepares responsible citizens for participation in a changing world, ensuring students develop positive self-esteem, respect for others, and a commitment to lifelong learning.

(Continued)

Figure 1.4 (Continued)

The Vision: What the WCSU Learning Community Will Look Like Five Years From Now

Curriculum, Instruction, and Assessment

- Student interests, needs, and strengths focus instruction.
- All curricula are aligned with standards and with classroom, school/district, and state assessments.
- Students have multiple opportunities to meet the standards through the following:
  - ○ Differentiated instruction corresponding to the learning opportunities described in the *Vermont Framework* and responding to the individual interests, strengths, and needs of students;
  - ○ Accommodations, modifications, interventions, extended learning opportunities that are available to help all students, including special populations, achieve the standards. Opportunities for advanced achievement, beyond the standards, are also provided, as appropriate.
  - ○ IEPs that directly address the standards and evidence in the *WCSU Curriculum and Assessment Plan.*
- Teachers consistently use research and data, independently and collaboratively, to inform instruction and meet the needs of individual students.
- Multiple and varied assessments are in place at the classroom and school/district levels to assess student progress toward meeting the standards and evidence.
- Teachers are skilled in using a variety of data to articulate student progress toward meeting the standards.
- A comprehensive assessment system provides classroom, school/district, and state measures of student learning, program effectiveness, and resource allocation (the WCSU Curriculum and Assessment Plan, the WCSU Student Assessment Profile, K–12 student report cards, school reports).
- Data from the WCSU comprehensive assessment system are used to inform decisions about planning, instructional and school improvement, and decisions about individual students (e.g., referrals, opportunities to learn, graduation).

School Climate

- The social and emotional welfare of our students is the foundation of their learning.
- Families and community members share with faculty, staff, and administration the collective responsibility for student well-being and improved student learning.
- School facilities are safe and accessible.
- All members of the school community make healthy choices and have accesses to health care resources.
- Partnerships with health and human services providers assure good health and improved learning in our schools.
- Each school is a safe, nurturing environment characterized by respect and is free from harassment, bullying, and violence in any form. Diversity is embraced in the WCSU learning community.
- The WCSU Comprehensive Assessment System includes data regarding vital results standards (including personal development and social responsibility standards), school climate, and student risk and asset factors.

Professional Development, Supervision, and Evaluation

- Educators and other staff members are valued through the investment of resources and supports from induction through career-long continuing development.
- All faculty, staff, administrators, and board members participate in ongoing learning and value their membership in the WCSU community of learners.
- Professional development opportunities are targeted to support standards implementation and positive school climate and to engage faculty, staff, and administration as a community of learners.
- A Professional Development Council creates and coordinates a long-term professional development plan that meets criteria for high quality professional development, including identification of staff needs.
- Job-embedded professional development opportunities are available to all teachers and administrators, including mentoring, colleague consultation, and peer coaching.
- Supervision and evaluation, relicensure, and action plans are aligned to provide a comprehensive system to support professional development of staff.

Community Partnerships/Communication With Students, Families, Staff, and Community and School Board Members

- Each student is known well by at least one adult in the school.
- Students receive regular feedback on their learning and on their progress toward meeting the standards.
- Student performance is reported to families two or more times annually.
- Family and community engagement is encouraged and facilitated.
- Student and school performance is reported to school boards and to the community annually.

District and School Resources and Policies for Continuous Improvement

- Policies at the school and district level support implementation of student-centered, standards-based education.
- Technology supports the implementation of standards-based education.
- Time for professional collaboration is provided.
- Budgets, planning, scheduling, federal and state grants, and human resources are aligned to support student performance in relation to the standards and evidence in the *WCSU Curriculum and Assessment Plan.*
- Budget development aligns with school/district action plans and with school and district goals.
- Additional resources, beyond local WCSU resources, are pursued to support the success of all students.
- WCSU consciously seeks to hire professional staff who are student-centered, are knowledgeable in the area(s) they teach, and who can apply best practices in standards-based instruction and assessment.
- Facilities, transportation, and ancillary services support school and community partnerships for improvement of learning of standards.
- Annual action plans and district strategic plans are reviewed and revised based on student results data (student performance data and other indicators, such as dropout rates), data about programs and practices, and data about resources.

Source: Washington Central Supervisory Union, VT. Used with permission.

Once the vision statement is completed, or even while it is in process, it is possible to begin to development of curriculum guidelines based on standards. Additional information is needed to clearly define the context of the work of the curriculum committee.

STATE AND FEDERAL MANDATES

State and federal mandates that impact curriculum must be taken into account throughout the development process. There is nothing worse than having a committee spend a year or more developing curriculum guidelines only to have them "fail" the next approval visit for lack of required components. Some states have very definite requirements for drug and alcohol education; some states promote inclusion of students with disability conditions in the regular classroom; and the No Child Left Behind legislation carries with it direct requirements for standards-based curriculum, instruction, and assessment across all subject areas.

Those on the committee may already be well aware of such mandates, but it is advisable to check to make sure that the latest versions of such requirements are being considered and included. It is worthwhile as well to write down the specific aspects of any mandates that apply to any particular curriculum development project. Worksheet 1.8, State and Federal Mandates, can be used for this purpose.

In addition, the committee should be supplied with standards and other resources pertinent to the curriculum development process.

Figure 1.5 Franklin Northeast Supervisory Union's Vision for Standards-Based Learning

---

Student-Centered, Standards-Based Education

The Vision: What the FNESU Learning Community Will Look Like in Five Years

> The Franklin Northeast Supervisory Union (FNESU) holds children and youth as the primary and obvious focus for all decisions and practices. School practices are clearly and directly aligned with current FNESU goals, which set high standards and high expectations for students, personnel, and parents. School practices ensure safe, learning-focused schools by maintaining positive environments and genuine learning opportunities for all students.

Curriculum, Instruction, and Assessment
- Student interests, needs, and strengths drive instruction.
  - Data from the FNESU comprehensive assessment system is used to inform decisions about planning, instructional and school improvement, and decisions about individual students (e.g., referrals, opportunities to learn, graduation.)
- Students have multiple opportunities to meet the standards through:
  - Instruction that corresponds to the learning opportunities described in the standards adopted by FNESU and responds to the individual interests, strengths, and needs of students;
  - Extended learning opportunities including accommodations, modifications, and interventions that are clearly articulated and available to help all students achieve the standards. Opportunities for advanced achievement, beyond the standards, are also provided. All teachers know what's available and who to go to get help.
  - IEPs that are consistent with the standards and evidence in the *FNESU Standards-Based Curriculum*.

School Climate
- The social and emotional welfare of our students is the foundation of their learning.
- Families and community members share with faculty, staff, and administration the collective responsibility for student well being and improved student learning.
- Each school strives to be a safe, nurturing environment characterized by respect and is free from harassment, bullying, and violence in any form. Diversity is embraced in the FNESU learning community.

Professional Development, Supervision, and Evaluation
- A Professional Development Council creates, coordinates, and communicates information about a long-term professional development plan that balances individual school needs, all schools' needs, and supervisory union opportunities and meets criteria for high quality professional development, including identification of staff needs through needs assessment.

Community Partnerships/Communication With Students, Families, Staff, and Community and School Board Members
- Each student is known well by at least one adult in the school.
- Students receive regular feedback on their learning and on their progress toward meeting the standards.

District and School Resources for Continuous Improvement
- Two-year action plans and district strategic plans are reviewed and revised annually based on student results data (student performance data and other indicators, such as dropout rates), data about programs and practices, and data about resources.

The Vision

The FNESU administrative team functions as a learning community focused on continuous improvement in the school district. Team members support each other by regularly sharing expertise and experience. The team actively explores and reflects upon new information, research and best practices particularly as those relate to curriculum, instruction, and assessment of student learning within the unified FNESU goals.

The FNESU Central Office will support school districts (schools, boards, employees, teachers, paraeducators, and administrators) and one another effectively and in a friendly manner. People in Central Office will maintain fiscal responsibility, respond to all questions, communicate and clarify information, produce accurate work, and maintain common direction across the district. At all times, Central Office personnel will maintain confidentiality.

Source: Franklin Northeast Supervisory Union, VT. Used with permission.

WORKSHEET 1.1 Evaluating Your Existing Vision Statement

Use the following checklist to examine your existing school's or district's vision statement. Ultimately, the statement should be one that all in the district refer to as the rationale for practices and decisions related to standards-based learning.

Yes	No	The Process of Development
___	___	Is the statement less than five years old?
___	___	Were teachers involved in developing the statement?
___	___	Were administrators involved in developing the statement?
___	___	Were parents and community members involved in developing or responding to the statement?
___	___	Were students involved in developing or responding to the statement?

Yes	No	The Content of the Vision
___	___	Are the beliefs and commitments clear about learners?
___	___	Are the beliefs and commitments clear about the focus on standards?
___	___	Are the beliefs and commitments clear about curriculum?
___	___	Are the beliefs and commitments clear about instruction?
___	___	Are the beliefs and commitments clear about assessment?
___	___	Are the beliefs and commitments clear about the use of data?
___	___	Are the beliefs and commitments clear about professional development?
___	___	Are the beliefs and commitments clear about supervision?
___	___	Are the beliefs and commitments clear about instructional leadership?

Yes	No	Communication of the Vision
___	___	Is the vision incorporated into the school's or district's Web site?
___	___	Is the vision referred to in meetings, curriculum development, and professional development sessions?

WORKSHEET 1.2 Reflections on a District Vision for Student-Centered, Standards-Based Learning

	Works for Us	Doesn't Work for Us	Need to Add
Learners			
Curriculum, instruction, and assessment			
School climate			
Professional development, supervision, and evaluation			
Community partnerships and communication with students, families, staff, and community and school board members			
District and school resources for continuous improvement			
Leadership			

Figure 1.6   Creating a Vision Statement

Creating a Vision Statement

If you find there is a need to revisit your school's or district's existing vision statement, or if you have no such statement and wish to create one from scratch, try using the following process.

1. Identify those who will be responsible for the process of gathering input and drafting the statement (Worksheet 1.3).

2. Distribute to all vision team members and to representative teachers, administrators, staff, school board members, parents, community members, and students the Vision Statement Input Form (Worksheet 1.4).

3. Collect the input forms and collate to identify primary themes, ideas, and phrases (Worksheet 1.5).

4. Have each team member take one section of the collated responses and create a draft for that section (Worksheet 1.6).

5. Put the drafts together, photocopy, and distribute to all team members. Discuss the draft, noting suggested revisions, additions, deletions, or other changes. Compare this draft to the district's previous philosophy or mission statement if one exists.

6. Have one or two team members take the resulting draft and write a complete draft for the team's review.

7. After the team has reviewed and agreed upon the draft, make it available to all those listed in Step 2 and solicit directed feedback (Worksheet 1.7).

8. Based on the feedback you receive, revise and finalize the draft.

9. Take the draft to the school board for adoption.

10. Publicize the vision statement!

SYNTHESIZING RESEARCH AND PROFESSIONAL RECOMMENDATIONS

For each subject area, there is a wealth of educational research suggesting, at least by implication, what ought to be included in district curriculum and how it should be taught. Professional organizations such as the National Council of Teachers of English, the National Council for the Social Studies, the National Council of Teachers of Mathematics, and others have produced numerous recommendations, resources, and examples relevant to the work of curriculum development committees.

It is not possible, of course, to read all the literature. Synthesizing the literature is rather like engaging in the process of writing: You spend time gathering ideas and information; you reach a point where no new ideas emerge; and then you write. What is important is that the committee is familiar with current curriculum issues within the discipline under development; is aware of recent recommendations, especially those regarding content, concepts, skills, and attitudes students need to learn and those regarding recommended instructional approaches and materials; and is willing to incorporate these in the final document.

We recommend conducting a computerized search to obtain key documents from the professional organizations that deal with the subject area in question, as well as having at least one or two local experts address the committee. Articles and chapters supplied by committee members (see Worksheet 4.2 in Chapter 4) are also important sources of this information.

Subcommittees can be used to produce short overviews. For example, a language arts committee might assign one subcommittee to each of the following areas: reading/literature, writing, listening/ speaking, and spelling/handwriting. Each subcommittee can then use Worksheet 1.9, Summarizing Research and Recommendations, to summarize results for the full committee. All completed sheets should be photocopied for each committee member.

WORKSHEET 1.3 District Vision Team

Instructions: List below pertinent information about the district vision team members. Each of the following groups should be represented on the team: teachers, administrators, staff, school board members, community members, parents, and students.

Name	School/Address	Telephone
1.		(w) (h)
2.		(w (h)
3.		(w) (h)
4.		(w) (h)
5.		(w) (h)
6.		(w) (h)
7.		(w) (h)
8.		(w) (h)

WORKSHEET 1.4 Vision Statement Input Form

Instructions: Please reflect on what you consider to be most essential to standards-based learning. On the form below, please write your response(s) to each of the open-ended statements. When you have finished, please return this sheet to _____ by _____.

I am a _____ teacher _____ administrator _____ staff member _____ parent _____ board member _____ community member _____ student at _____ School

Learners are _____

_____

_____

_____

_____

The purpose of standards in the _____

district is _____

_____

_____

_____

_____

Students learn best when _____

_____

_____

_____

Assessment of student learning should _____

_____

_____

_____

Teachers should _____

_____

_____

_____

Administrators should _____

_____

_____

_____

Parents and community members should _____

_____

_____

_____

WORKSHEET 1.5 Collating Vision Statement Input Responses

List below the major themes, ideas, and phrases that resulted from your review of the Vision Statement Input forms you received. Use a separate sheet for each "lead" statement on the Input form.

Lead: _____

Themes/ideas/phrases: _____

_____

_____

_____

_____

_____

_____

_____

_____

WORKSHEET 1.6 Vision Statement Draft

_____

_____

_____

_____

_____

_____

_____

_____

_____

_____

WORKSHEET 1.7 Vision Feedback Form

The _____ District Vision Statement Team has used your input to create a draft of the vision statement that will guide all educational efforts in the coming years. We need your help! Use the form below to let us know what you think of the attached draft. Feel free to write any recommended changes right on the draft. Please return this form and the philosophy or mission statement draft on which you have written revisions to

_____   by _____.
(Person)   (Date)

What should we keep?

What should we add?

What should we change?

What should we delete?

Additional comments:

WORKSHEET 1.8 State and Federal Mandates

Note below any specific mandates that apply to the curriculum area you are about to develop (e.g., mathematics). What requirements must be met as you conduct this curriculum work? When finished, photocopy this sheet and distribute to all committee members.

State mandates:

Federal mandates:

WORKSHEET 1.9 Summarizing Research and Recommendations

After reviewing relevant research and recommendations for the area you have been assigned, record key findings in the space below.

Area: _____

Key issues in this curriculum area are:

Content that should be emphasized in a curriculum document for this curriculum area is:

Concepts that should be emphasized in a curriculum document for this curriculum area are:

Skills that should be emphasized in a curriculum document for this curriculum area are:

Recommended instructional approaches are:

Recommended instructional materials are:

Recommended approaches to classroom assessment are:

Some curriculum teams prefer to summarize the research in the form of a checklist that can then be used to analyze the existing local curriculum. Figure 1.7 shows a sample mathematics checklist that can be used to analyze existing curriculum in the district.

ANALYZING EXISTING CURRICULUM IN THE DISTRICT

An essential early step in the development of standards-based curriculum guidelines is to analyze the existing curriculum in the district. Existing curriculum guides are one relevant source of information, but even more important is the actual curriculum in the district—that which is being taught across grade levels and schools. Gathering this information will allow the curriculum development committee to uncover unintentional gaps and overlaps, to acknowledge existing practices while making decisions about the new scope and sequence and instructional guidelines, to determine areas most in need of staff development, and to identify the null curriculum in the district. This is an important base from which to consider related educational research literature and recommendations of relevant professional organizations.

Have departments and grade level teams across the district complete Worksheet 1.10, Gathering District Curriculum Data. Working together, teachers can complete this task during department meets or by breaking into small groups during a faculty meeting. The forms are then returned to a committee representative by a specified date.

Once all teachers in the district have completed Worksheet 1.10, it is necessary to compile the data in order to achieve a cumulative view of what is taught at each grade level. Worksheet 1.11 is provided for this purpose.

An alternative way to accomplish this task is to cover a wall of the curriculum development committee meeting room using large strips of butcher paper, reproduce the grid found in Worksheet 1.11 and expand it to represent each grade, and have committee members fill in the information provided by teams and departments of district teachers using Worksheet 1.10. This is more fun, and it quickly results in a graphic representation of the curriculum across grade levels throughout the district. Converting the chart to a table or spreadsheet on the computer is the most efficient way to compile the data.

The next step is to analyze the taught curriculum using the series of questions provided on Worksheet 1.12, Identifying Curriculum Overlaps and Inconsistencies. What overlaps exist?

For example, a mathematics committee we once worked with was surprised to discover that in all schools manipulative activities were used exclusively through grade three and that in grade four all teachers relied entirely on textbooks for instruction. This suggested that no transition was being provided for students and that this was an issue that needed to be addressed in the curriculum guidelines they produced. A social studies committee discovered that the topic of dinosaurs was being taught in some classrooms at four different grade levels but was not being taught in other classrooms at any of these grade levels. Thus, some students were studying this topic several times, while others were not studying it at all. They decided that this represented both a potential undesirable gap and undesirable overlap and needed to be addressed through the work they were doing. A language arts committee discovered that teachers across all grade levels were teaching writing as a process. This was deemed to be a desirable overlap within the taught curriculum.

The final step is to compare your curriculum analysis, Worksheet 1.11, to the completed Worksheet 1.9, Summarizing Research and Recommendations, to decide what's missing, what areas need to be refocused, and what areas will require staff development. Use Worksheet 1.13, Identifying Curriculum Gaps, for this purpose.

The processes described in this chapter can be undertaken either prior to or concurrent with the actual development of the curriculum guidelines. If you have not yet begun that process, you are now ready to do so.

Figure 1.7 Mathematics Checklist

Mathematics Checklist

By Jennifer Blasdell, Dana Fatone, Matt Mitchell, and Jaime Kisner

Curriculum	Yes	No	Notes
Standard-based			
Targets problem solving, reasoning, critical thinking			
Incorporates technology			
Clearly stated and defined objectives			
Comprehensive			
Includes real-life applications			
Provides training for teachers			
Standards are organized and sequential			
Differentiated for all learners			

Instruction	Yes	No	Notes
Strengthens problem solving, reasoning, critical thinking			
Meets needs of all learners			
Incorporates technology			
Student-centered			
Incorporates cooperative learning			
Provide wait time			
Hands-on activities			
Varied question forms, higher-order thinking skills			
Provide visual representations			
Tools used • Calculator • Ruler • Protractor • Manipulatives			
Modeling, guided practice, independent work			

Assessment	Yes	No	Notes
Open-ended assessment			
Feedback provided (by teacher and student)			
Informal assessment			
Formal assessment			
Multiple types • Portfolio • Writing • Project			
Based upon standards taught			
Custom made for students			

WORKSHEET 1.10 Gathering District Curriculum Data

The _____ Curriculum Development Committee is in the process of developing new curriculum guidelines for the district. In order to do so, we need a clear picture of what is actually being taught in the district now. Please take a few minutes to respond to the questions below. Please complete a separate sheet for each grade level or, where appropriate in the case of a high school, for each course.

Grade Level: Subject Area: School:

1. What topics are taught and assessed?

2. What skills do students learn each year?

3. What concepts do students learn each year?

4. What materials do you use to teach these topics, skills, and content to your students?

5. What instructional approaches (lecture, discussion, cooperative groups, role playing, etc.) do you use predominantly during the year?

6. What standards are taught and assessed during the year? (Please attach.)

WORKSHEET 1.11   Compiling District Curriculum Data

Sort completed Worksheets 1.10, Gathering District Curriculum Data, into piles by grade level and school. Have individuals or pairs of committee members take responsibility for compiling the data for one or two grade levels. Use a separate sheet for each grade level and use more than one sheet if necessary. List by school the topics, concepts, and skills taught at each grade level, as well as the materials used, the instructional approaches favored, and the types of classroom assessment used. Also identify the standards that have been appended. Converting this chart to a computer table or spreadsheet makes the work most efficient.

	School: _____	School: _____	School: _____
Topics			
Skills			
Concepts			
Materials			
Teaching approaches			
Standards			

WORKSHEET 1.12 Identifying Curriculum Overlaps and Inconsistencies

As a group, analyze the results of Worksheet 1.11 to respond to the following questions. Write your responses below.

1. What topics are repeated across grade levels?

2. What skills are repeated across grade levels?

3. What concepts are repeated across grade levels?

4. What inconsistencies exist with regard to materials used?

5. What inconsistencies exist with regard to instructional approaches used?

6. What inconsistencies exist with regard to the standards that are taught and assessed?

WORKSHEET 1.13   Identifying Curriculum Gaps and Consistencies

Compare the results of Worksheet 1.11, Compiling District Curriculum Data, to the results of Worksheet 1.9, Summarizing Research and Recommendations. Discuss what is missing from the taught curriculum that is recommended in the educational literature and by professional organizations. Also discuss consistencies you discover that indicate aspects of the taught curriculum that should be kept in the new curriculum guidelines. Note these below.

Curriculum Gaps:

Curriculum Consistencies:

2

Establishing a Curriculum Development, Implementation, and Evaluation Cycle

If standards are to have the desired impact on student learning, they will do so only because of what happens for and with students in the classroom. If there is to be a reasonable degree of match among the written curriculum, the actual experiences provided in classrooms and schools, and what students learn, curriculum must become an ongoing, almost an organic, process within the school district. In this way all professional staff members and selected community members are engaged in a continuous, dynamic dialogue about what is taught and what is learned; everyone is more open to means of improving classroom practice; and students benefit. Questions to be answered in developing a curriculum cycle are listed in Figure 2.1.

It takes time to develop curriculum guidelines, to implement them, and to assess them. During that time, the knowledge base of any discipline may increase, new and better approaches to instruction may be validated in the professional literature, new teachers and administrators may be hired in the district, community values may shift, and so on.

Designing a curriculum cycle ensures that when new curriculum guidelines are created, the reaction won't be "There, we won't have to worry about that for another 15 years," but rather "How are we going to make this work?" It makes curriculum a living process, one that responds to the needs of teachers and learners. And it creates an awareness for all involved that curriculum revision and improvement will take place regularly.

This chapter provides the basis for the creation of a curriculum development, implementation, and evaluation cycle that involves five considerations, as shown in Figure 2.2. Figure 2.3 provides instructions for designing a curriculum process in your district. Worksheet 2.1 can be used to record information about the curriculum process design team.

Figure 2.1 Questions to Be Answered in Developing a Curriculum Cycle

- Why design a cycle of development, implementation, and evaluation?
- What is the purpose of the K–12 curriculum process?
- What definition of curriculum will be used?
- What are the beliefs and preferences of the community with regard to curriculum?
- How will consistency be provided across curriculum areas (e.g., format)?
- What are the priorities?
- What is the timeline?
- Who is responsible for what?

Figure 2.2 Establishing a Curriculum Process

1. Defining curriculum

2. Identifying purposes

3. Adopting a curriculum process model

4. Defining context

5. Establishing priorities and timelines

Figure 2.3 Designing a Curriculum Process

1. Identify those who will have responsibility for designing the curriculum process. List them on Worksheet 2.1.

2. Provide each participant with copies of all materials from this chapter.

3. Review the worksheets with the participants.

4. Work through the five steps in designing a curriculum process one at a time. For each, review background information, complete worksheets provided, discuss, and reach consensus. Repeat this process for each worksheet in each section.

TAKING RESPONSIBILITY

Who will make decisions about what the curriculum process in the district will be? It is critical that roles and responsibilities be clearly established at the outset and that they be taken on willingly by those involved. Three approaches are most common: (1) One person, most often a curriculum coordinator, assistant superintendent, or superintendent, designs the process; (2) the entire administrative team for the district designs the process; or (3) a curriculum process design team designs the process.

If a design team is used, it can be composed of one or more teachers, administrators, board members, or community members. It is best to keep this committee small, say three to five individuals, in order to facilitate communication and progress within the group. The advantages and disadvantages of each of these approaches are shown in Figure 2.4.

WORKSHEET 2.1 Curriculum Process Design Team

List below the name, position, school, and phone numbers for each member of the curriculum process design team. Photocopy the completed sheet and give a copy to each member of the team.

Name	Position	School	Phone
1.			(h) (w)
2.			(h) (w)
3.			(h) (w)
4.			(h) (w)
5.			(h) (w)

Figure 2.4 Approaches to Taking Responsibility: Advantages and Disadvantages

Approach	Advantages	Disadvantages
One person	• Control of the process is centralized • Takes less time	• Those who will be involved feel lack of ownership
Administrative team	• All schools are included	• Teachers are left out
Curriculum process design team	• All constituencies can be represented	• Takes more time

Whichever approach is used, it must be determined who is responsible for seeing that specific tasks are accomplished and who needs to be involved in each task. Worksheet 2.2 can be used for making these determinations.

DEFINING CURRICULUM

Educators involved in curriculum development often make statements like the following:

- "I have to cover . . ."
- "I don't have time to cover . . ."
- "The district expects me to cover . . .
- "The state thinks I can cover . . ."

These statements come from those who define curriculum as what is taught. Others define curriculum as what is learned, and they are more likely to focus on questions such as "What is important for students to learn?" "How do they best learn it?" and "How will we know what they have learned?" Before designing a curriculum cycle, it is critical to determine which of these definitions will be the basis of the effort and to understand its implications. Each carries with it a different focus. Figure 2.5 distinguishes these two definitions.

Figure 2.5 The Focus of Curriculum

What is taught	What is learned
Coverage	Meaning
Teacher-centered	Student-centered
Teaching	Learning
Passive	Active
Judgment	Feedback
Topics	Standards

WORKSHEET 2.2 Taking Responsibility for Design of the Curriculum Process

As a group, discuss who will take responsibility for each of the tasks listed on this sheet. Also determine who else needs to be involved. Record your decisions below.

	Person Responsible	Others Who Need to Be Involved
Defining curriculum		
Identifying purposes		
Adopting a curriculum model		
Defining context		
Establishing priorities and timelines		

The decision made about the focus of the curriculum has implications for how the curriculum is designed, implemented, and ultimately evaluated. In a standards-based system, the focus is on what is learned. This increases the importance of feedback to students about their learning in relation to standards. It also means that the essential evaluation of the curriculum has to do with the extent to which students know and can do what learning (goals, objectives, and performance indicators) presented in the scope-and-sequence document.

Those involved in designing the curriculum cycle need to determine at the outset their own shared definition of *curriculum*. Worksheet 2.3 can be used for this purpose.

ADOPTING A CURRICULUM PROCESS MODEL

Once you have defined what you mean by the term curriculum, it is useful to observe that the term is used in different ways to refer to many types of processes and products at different levels. It is important to identify different levels of curriculum (Goodlad & Associates, 1979; Rogers & Stevenson, 1988) and to establish the relationships of one level to another. These will become the basis for the development of your curriculum process model.

At the highest level, an *ideal curriculum* is that represented by educational research or proposed by professional organizations such as the National Science Foundation and the National Council of Teachers of English. Such proposals represent a curriculum ideal for a discipline, although they are rarely implemented in their pure form by school districts.

A *national curriculum* means curricular expectations and mandates formally articulated by some countries, such as Great Britain, that are to be addressed by all schools. While the United States does not have such a document at this time, there are some who believe that the rampant use of standardized tests and textbooks produced by publishers is a de facto form of national curriculum. Special education laws represent federally mandated expectations that affect curriculum.

State-mandated curricula, which are being adopted in an ever-growing number of states, apply to all school districts throughout the state. State standards for student learning, now adopted by all states except Iowa, are one form of state-mandated curricula.

District curriculum guidelines are meant to be implemented across all schools in a given district and usually take the form of K–12 curriculum guidelines.

School curriculum guides or courses of study are created by individual schools to expand upon the district's K–12 curriculum guidelines. If the K–12 curriculum guidelines are presented in grade-level blocks, for example, the school curriculum guide may more specifically state expectations for each grade level. Lists of actual materials and resources available for implementing the curriculum guidelines in the particular school may be included. Some schools also keep on file sample units of study developed by teachers to provide concrete examples of implementation.

The *teacher's curriculum* varies from classroom to classroom as teachers implement district guidelines and school curriculum guides in their own ways. Plans are based on the teacher's perceptions of what is expected by the school, school district, state, and nation; on the teacher's beliefs about students and learning; and on the teacher's own knowledge and experience.

The *student curriculum* reflects the fact that each student perceives the curriculum in a unique way. The needs and strengths, as well as the prior experiences and learning, of individual students influence how students experience learning activities and opportunities provided throughout the year.

The *learned curriculum* is students' actual knowledge, understandings, abilities, and attitudes learned.

The *null curriculum* (Eisner, 1985) is what is not taught. When we focus exclusively on the history and political thought of Western civilizations, for example, that of Asia or third world countries becomes the null curriculum because it is ignored.

WORKSHEET 2.3 Defining Curriculum

This worksheet should be completed individually by each member of the planning group. On each continuum below, place an *x* at the point that best represents what the curriculum is in practice in the district. Place an *o* on each continuum at the point that best represents what the curriculum ought to be.

The focus is on:

What is taught ———————————————————————— What is learned

Coverage ——————————————————————————— Meaning

Teacher-centered ———————————————————— Student-centered

Teaching ——————————————————————————— Learning

Passive ————————————————————————————— Active

Judgment ——————————————————————————— Feedback

Topics ——————————————————————————————— Standards

As a group, discuss individual placements on each continuum.

- Is the district's definition in practice what you desire it to be?
- What is your group's definition of curriculum?

Write your definition below:

_____

_____

_____

_____

_____

Figure 2.6 A Curriculum Process Model

```
┌──────────────────────────────────────────────────────────────────────────┐
│        ┌────────────────────────────────────────────────────┐             │
│        │              DISTRICT VISION STATEMENT              │             │
│        └────────────────────────────────────────────────────┘             │
│                                                                            │
│  ┌──────────────────┐  ┌──────────────────┐  ┌──────────────────┐         │
│  │      IDEAL       │  │  NATIONAL/STATE  │  │ EXISTING DISTRICT │        │
│  │   CURRICULUM     │  │   CURRICULUM     │  │    CURRICULUM     │         │
│  │                  │  │                  │  │                   │         │
│  │ • Educational    │  │ • Standards      │  │ • Guidelines      │         │
│  │   Research       │  │ • Regulations    │  │ • Teachers'       │         │
│  │ • Professional   │  │ • Laws           │  │ • Hidden          │         │
│  │   Organizations  │  │                  │  │ • Null            │         │
│  └──────────────────┘  └──────────────────┘  └──────────────────┘         │
│                                                                            │
│       ┌──────────────────────────────────────────────────────┐           │
│       │            K–12 CURRICULUM GUIDELINES                 │           │
│       │                                                        │          │
│       │ • Purpose            • Instructional Guidelines       │           │
│       │ • Goals              • Needs and Recommendations      │           │
│       │ • Scope and Sequence • Program Evaluation Statement   │           │
│       └──────────────────────────────────────────────────────┘           │
│                                                                            │
│  ┌──────────────────┐  ┌──────────────────┐  ┌──────────────────┐         │
│  │   PROFESSIONAL   │  │  DEVELOPMENTAL   │  │     MENTORING,    │        │
│  │   DEVELOPMENT    │  │   SUPERVISION    │  │   COACHING, AND   │         │
│  │                  │  │                  │  │ COLLEAGUE SUPPORT │         │
│  └──────────────────┘  └──────────────────┘  └──────────────────┘         │
│                                                                            │
│  ┌──────────────────────────────────────────────────────────────┐        │
│  │              THE IMPLEMENTED CURRICULUM                        │        │
│  │                                                                │        │
│  │ • Teachers' Perceived Curriculum  • Students' Experienced Curriculum │ │
│  │ • The Taught Curriculum           • The Assessed Curriculum    │       │
│  │                                   • The Learned Curriculum     │       │
│  └──────────────────────────────────────────────────────────────┘        │
│                                                                            │
│  ┌──────────────────────────────────────────────────────────────┐        │
│  │                   PROGRAM EVALUATION                           │        │
│  │                                                                │        │
│  │ • Are the goals of the curriculum being achieved?             │        │
│  │ • Does the curriculum need to be revised?                     │        │
│  └──────────────────────────────────────────────────────────────┘        │
└──────────────────────────────────────────────────────────────────────────┘
```

The *hidden curriculum* (Giroux and Purpel, 1983) is what is taught unintentionally or covertly; it is not made explicit. Students learn much simply from the way they are treated in school. For example, students who work in groups can learn to cooperate, while those who work mostly alone often do not learn to work in a collaborative fashion.

Figure 2.6 is a recursive curriculum model that reflects the interrelationships of these levels of curriculum. Please review the model before moving onto the next section, Identifying Purposes.

IDENTIFYING PURPOSES

How extensive the cycle is and what is included depend in large part on the purposes the district has for the K–12 curriculum process. Within any district, the K–12 curriculum process may serve one or many purposes, as shown in Figure 2.7.

Districts differ in the relative emphasis they place on each of these purposes. Those involved in designing the curriculum cycle should jointly decide which of these purposes are most important. Worksheet 2.4, Identifying and Prioritizing Curriculum Purposes, should be used by those involved

Figure 2.7 Purpose of the K–12 Curriculum Process

- Provide direction for a school system
- Assure all students in all subgroups have opportunities to attain all standards
- Articulate community values
- Establish common goals and expectations across schools in the district
- Provide context for communication about curriculum
- Provide basis for addressing individual students' needs
- Coordinate instruction
- Provide basis for decision making (budget, scheduling, personnel allocations)
- Ensure consistency and continuity of educational opportunities
- Establish context for program assessment
- Provide a vehicle for school improvement
- Comply with state and federal standards

in designing the curriculum cycle to determine which purposes have the highest priority for curriculum development, implementation, and assessment in the district.

Now go back to the curriculum process model shown in Figure 2.6. Given the purposes you have identified as top priorities, which components of the model will be most important to emphasize in your curriculum process? Indicate these on the model by placing an asterisk inside each box in the diagram that represents an area you intend to emphasize. You may wish to formally adopt the model and distribute it throughout the district.

THE CURRICULUM CONTEXT

Significant forces in the district's environment need to be identified prior to designing a curriculum process. Three kinds of forces create the curriculum environment, as shown on Figure 2.8. It is important to recognize these forces and to develop specific plans to utilize the positive forces and

Figure 2.8 Environmental Forces

Social

- What are the socioeconomic realities in the district?
- Who are the significant individuals in the school and community?
- How do these individuals relate to one another?

Political

- What is the role of the school board?
- What is the role of the teachers' union?
- What religious or liberal/conservative interest groups exist in the community? What role do they play?

Historical

- What has been the district's curriculum experience?
- What has been the district's experience with standards to date?
- What is the public's perception of the school?

WORKSHEET 2.4 Identifying and Prioritizing Curriculum Purposes

Below is a list of purposes for the curriculum process. As a group, identify any additional purposes that apply in your district and write them in the space provided. Then, individually, rank the purposes of curriculum using the form below (1 = high priority; 13 = low priority).

Purposes of the K–12 Curriculum Process

Rank Purpose

____ Provide direction for a school system

____ Assure all students in all subgroups have opportunities to attain all standards

____ Articulate community values

____ Establish common goals and expectations

____ Provide context for communication about curriculum

____ Provide basis for addressing individual students' needs

____ Coordinate instruction

____ Provide basis for decision making

____ Ensure consistency and continuity of educational opportunities

____ Establish context for program assessment

____ Provide a vehicle for school improvement

____ Comply with state and federal mandates

____Other: _____

____Other: _____

____Other: _____

Next, use a blank worksheet to record the numbers assigned each purpose by each individual involved in the process. Add up each group of numbers and divide by the total number of responses to get the group's ranking of each purpose for the K–12 curriculum process.

counteract the negative ones throughout the curriculum process. Use Worksheets 2.5, 2.6, and 2.7 for this purpose.

ASSESSING NEEDS AND ESTABLISHING PRIORITIES

In districts where there has been no systematic curriculum cycle in place, there is typically little or no reliable assessment information on which to base decisions about where to start or what to change. In the absence of such information, it is necessary to conduct a needs assessment to determine perceived needs as they relate to curriculum. (If you have already been through a process of curriculum development, implementation, and assessment and have available program evaluation information, skip the needs assessment and use the program evaluation information instead. See Chapter 10, Curriculum-Based Program Evaluation, for more information.)

Figure 2.9 describes the process for conducting the needs assessment. Worksheet 2.8 is a needs assessment questionnaire. This worksheet includes disciplines that have traditionally been addressed in curriculum work. This should be modified, as needed, to reflect the curriculum areas your district actually intends to develop. For example, if the focus is interdisciplinary guidelines for such areas as communication, problem solving, and global stewardship, these areas should be listed on the needs assessment questionnaire you distribute. Worksheet 2.9 can be used to collate the results of your needs assessment, and Worksheet 2.10 is provided for your use in identifying priority areas for development.

Figure 2.9 Needs Assessment Process

1. Distribute Worksheet 2.8 to all administrators and a sample of representative teachers in the district. You may also wish to have representatives of the following groups complete the worksheet: parents, board members, community members, students. If so, color code the sheets to make it easier to collate the responses of each group.

2. Collect all worksheets.

3. Use Worksheet 2.9 to collate information for each item.

4. Identify high, medium, and low priorities for curriculum development using Worksheet 2.10.

DEVELOPING A TIMELINE

Now that you have identified the individuals responsible for creating the curriculum cycle, identified curriculum purposes, adopted a curriculum model, defined the curriculum context, and assessed your needs, it is time to establish a timeline for the development, implementation, and assessment of each curriculum area.

You will, in general, find the following:

- Language arts, math, science, and social studies take the most time to develop.
- Teachers who teach multiple subjects can only start implementation of one new curriculum document in a given year.
- Resources need to be distributed across time.

WORKSHEET 2.5 Identifying Forces That Influence the Curriculum

Give each individual involved in designing the district's curriculum process a copy of this worksheet. Individually, respond to the questions below.

Social Forces

1. What social forces (demographics, relationships in the school and community) are most likely to negatively impact the curriculum development process in the district?

2. What social forces are most likely to positively impact the curriculum development process in the district?

Political Forces

1. What political forces (school board, teachers' union, interest groups) are most likely to negatively impact the curriculum development process in the district?

2. What political forces are most likely to positively impact the curriculum development process in the district?

Historical Forces

1. What historical forces (curriculum history, perceptions about curriculum) are most likely to negatively impact the curriculum development process in the district?

2. What historical forces are most likely to positively impact the curriculum development process in the district?

WORKSHEET 2.6 **The Curriculum Context**

Complete this worksheet following discussion of Worksheet 2.5. Use this page to record your consensus regarding the forces that negatively and positively influence curriculum in your district.

Negative Force   *Positive Force*

WORKSHEET 2.7 Addressing Forces That Influence the Curriculum

For each negative force identified on Worksheet 1.6, generate a list of one to three ways to counteract or respond to the force.

Negative Force   *Ways to Counteract*

For each positive force identified on Worksheet 2.6, generate a list of one to three ways to utilize the force.

Positive Force   *Ways to Utilize*

WORKSHEET 2.8 Needs Assessment Questionnaire

The _____ District Curriculum Team is in the process of designing a timeline for curriculum development for the district. We need your help! Please complete the following questionnaire and return it to

_____ by _____.
(Person)   (Date)

Please put a check to indicate whether you are a
_____ Teacher _____ Parent _____ Administrator _____ Board Member
_____ Community Member _____ Student

After each area of the curriculum listed below, please indicate whether you consider the area to be a high, medium, or low priority for curriculum development at this time. (1 = high priority, 2 = medium priority, 3 = low priority)

	Priority		
	Low	Medium	High
Art	1	2	3
Computers/technology	1	2	3
Health	1	2	3
Home economics	1	2	3
English/language arts	1	2	3
Mathematics	1	2	3
Music	1	2	3
Physical education	1	2	3
Social studies	1	2	3
Technology education/industrial arts	1	2	3
Integrated curriculum	1	2	3
Other: _____	1	2	3
Other: _____	1	2	3

Thank you for your help.

WORKSHEET 2.9 Collating Needs Assessment Results

Use this worksheet to collate needs assessment results.

	1	2	3
Art			
Computers/technology			
Health			
Home economics			
English/language arts			
Mathematics			
Music			
Physical education			
Social studies			
Technology education/industrial arts			
Integrated curriculum			
Other: _____			
Other: _____			

WORKSHEET 2.10 Identifying Priority Areas for Development

Based on the results of Worksheet 2.9, record high, medium, and low priorities for curriculum development.

High	Medium	Low

Therefore, even if your needs assessment suggests that mathematics, science, and language arts are high-priority areas for development, it is not wise to begin development of all three areas in the same year. At the same time, given the large number of curriculum areas that need to be developed by most school districts, it is not realistic to begin development of only one area each year because the length of time between development and revision of any one area would then be far too long to be effective. Review Figure 2.10, a sample timeline that demonstrates decisions made as a result of considering priorities and constraints. Then use Worksheet 2.11 to develop your own timeline for curriculum development, implementation, and evaluation across curricular areas.

Having established a cycle of curriculum development, implementation, and assessment, you are now ready to get started with the first curriculum area. The materials in the remainder of this book can be used as you go through the process in any curriculum area, and they may be used over and over again as you address additional areas of the curriculum.

Figure 2.10 Sample Curriculum Timeline

D = Development		I = Implementation			E = Evaluation	
	Year 1	*Year 2*	*Year 3*	*Year 4*	*Year 5*
Language arts	D	D I	I	I	E
Library/media	D	I	I	E	D
Math		D	I	I	I
Computers		D	I	I	E
Science			D	I	I
Health			D	I	I
Social studies				D	I
Fine arts				D	I
PE					D
Home economics					D

WORKSHEET 2.11 **Creating a Curriculum Timeline**

D = Development   I = Implementation   E = Evaluation

Year 1   Year 2   Year 3   Year 4   Year 5

3

Preparing for Committee Meetings

Once you have defined curriculum and identified your purposes for establishing a curriculum development, implementation, and assessment cycle, created a timeline, and identified who's responsible for what, you are ready to deal with the details that need to be addressed before the curriculum committee meets for the first time. This chapter will help you clarify the following:

- The charge to the committee
- On what basis committees will be formed
- Who will participate
- When and where meetings will take place
- Who will be the chairperson

Before the first committee meeting, you will also identify and budget for resources that will be needed.

THE CHARGE TO THE COMMITTEE

When seeking committee members, it is necessary to state exactly what it is they are being asked to do. If the work of the committee is ultimately to be productive, all members must know precisely what the task is. The charge to the committee should come from the individuals who have taken responsibility for designing the curriculum process—the superintendent, the administrative team, or an entire curriculum process design team. Worksheet 3.1 can be used to develop the charge to the committee.

WORKSHEET 3.1 **The Charge to the Curriculum Development Committee**

It is important that the task of the curriculum development committee be absolutely clear from the outset. In response to the questions below, record what the committee's charge is.

What area of the curriculum is to be addressed (e.g., English, language arts)?

What components of this area of the curriculum must be included (e.g., reading, writing, listening, speaking)?

What standards, performance indicators, or grade-level expectations must be incorporated?

What must be included in the curriculum guidelines? (See Chapter 5.)

Is there a specified format? (See Chapter 6.)

SELECTING COMMITTEE MEMBERS

If the K–12 curriculum guidelines are to be of high quality, accepted by teachers across the district, and ultimately implemented in classrooms, it is important that the curriculum committee be representative of the makeup of the district. But in forming a committee, you must balance the need for representation with the need to keep the committee a reasonable size to get the job done. Committees of 7 to 10 members are usually the most efficient; committees larger than 15 are often unwieldy.

If practicable, each school in the district should be represented, as should each level of schooling: primary (K–2), intermediate (3–5), middle grades (6–8), and high school (9–12). Teachers and administrators should serve on the committee; you may wish to include a community member or two; and it is worthwhile to have teachers who are both less and more experienced on the committee. Those who are not "regular" classroom teachers (e.g., special educators, the enrichment coordinator) and at least one teacher whose primary teaching responsibility is in a different curriculum area can bring useful perspectives to the process.

Individuals representing varied philosophies and assumptions should participate. For example, if some teachers in the district work from a developmental perspective, some are more comfortable with an outcomes-based approach, and some are very subject-centered, it is important that all three perspectives be represented on the committee. This will help to ensure that the product of the committee's work will be more readily accepted by all teachers who will be responsible for implementing the guidelines.

It is equally important to balance representatives who have recently served on other curriculum development committees with those who have not. There are those in every district who like to be involved in everything, but overreliance on only a small core of individuals to develop curriculum across curriculum areas can lead to a sense within the district that the process is not a truly representative one, that if you're not in the "in" group, your ideas don't count, or that the administration plays favorites.

You must also decide whether the committee will be made up entirely of volunteers, if you will appoint some or all members, or if you will work with a combination of volunteers or appointees. We favor a combination of volunteers and appointees for several reasons. We believe that, if possible, anyone who volunteers should be given the opportunity to participate and that a general solicitation should be sent out requesting that teachers and administrators volunteer. Worksheet 3.2 can be used to solicit volunteers for the committee.

It is critical though for those in the district who are seen as particularly influential in the curriculum area to be included, and this cannot be left entirely to chance. Also those who have strong opinions—either positive or negative—about the area of the curriculum in question should be included. Involving them in the process will help to ensure that they will actively support the work of the committee during the implementation phase. Finally, including at least one individual who has served on an earlier curriculum committee for the same curriculum area provides an important link with the past and reinforces the idea that curriculum is a process.

Worksheet 3.3 can be used to identify essential individuals you wish to ask to serve on the committee. You'll want to contact those you select in person or by phone to make your request.

When individuals you've invited have agreed to serve on the committee and other individuals have volunteered, be sure to cross-check to make sure the committee is representative. Use the matrix in Figure 3.1 to assess your list of committee members. Have you achieved a balanced committee?

CHOOSING A COMMITTEE CHAIRPERSON

Who will chair the committee? A member of the curriculum process design team, the curriculum coordinator, or a respected district teacher can chair the committee. What is more important than the

WORKSHEET 3.2 Soliciting Volunteers for Curriculum Development

Fill in the blanks in the memorandum below or type and distribute.

To:

From:

Date:

Re: Formation of the _____ Curriculum Development Committee.

The _____ School District is about to embark on development of new _____ K–12, standards-based curriculum guidelines. Volunteers to serve on the committee are needed. Please contact me at _____ if you would like more information or to sign up.

Thank you.

Figure 3.1   Balancing Committee Membership

Schools	#1		#2	#3	#4	#5		#6	#7
Grade Levels	K–2			3–5		6–8			9–12
Roles	Teacher				Administrator			Other	
Philosophies/ Assumptions	Developmental				Outcomes-Based			Subject-Centered	
Experience	0–5 Years					6+ Years			
Prior Committee Involvement	Yes					No			
Influential	Yes					No			
Opinionated	Positive					Negative			

individual's professional role in the district, however, is that the person selected has the necessary characteristics to be the committee chair. Above all, the committee chair must be highly organized and have strong human relations skills. It is best when the chairperson is perceived by those on the committee to be unbiased and fair.

Some committees select their own chair. The danger in this approach is that the person identified for this important role may not have the necessary skills and characteristics to lead such a complex effort. On the other hand, in committees that opt to work without a chair or decide to rotate that role, we have noticed that the individual who has the necessary skills usually emerges as a leader in the process, even if no such formal designation is made.

The chair of the committee needs to prepare for the role. Chapter 4 of this book provides specific information on group dynamics and running meetings.

COMMITTEE LOGISTICS

When will committee meetings take place? After school? Evenings? Saturdays? In the summer? Inservice? Released time? Will you use synchronous or asynchronous committee meetings, electronic document exchange, Webcasts, and so forth? Some on your initial list of committee members may not be able to participate at the times you select, and it is important to know at the outset if this is the case. There are advantages and disadvantages to each option for meeting times, as shown in Figure 3.2.

The length of time between meetings is another critical factor. When meetings take place weekly, less time at each meeting needs to be spent "getting back up to speed," but weekly meetings are usually relatively short, and less gets done at each one. Longer meetings once a month or so allow more to be done at each meeting, but the momentum of the previous meeting can be lost before it is time for the next one. It is also true that the later hours of a full-day meeting are less productive than the earlier ones.

Specific considerations within your own district should be factored in as well. On what afternoons do staff meetings take place in each of the schools? How are inservice days used? Is money available to pay summer stipends or to pay substitutes in order to release teachers during the school day?

WORKSHEET 3.3 **Identifying Essential Committee Members**

Brainstorm below a list of individuals who are influential within the district in the curriculum area to be developed.

Brainstorm below a list of individuals in the district who are very opinionated about this area of the curriculum.

Of those listed on your brainstormed lists, whose participation is most critical on the curriculum development committee? List those individuals below.

Figure 3.2   Meeting Times: Advantages and Disadvantages

Time	Advantages	Disadvantages
After school	• Availability of members • Possible to meet regularly	• Lack of time • Fatigue of members • Conflicts with other meetings and commitments (e.g., child care)
Evenings	• Provides break before meeting • Possible to meet regularly	• Fatigue of members • Those who live far away may not want to return
Saturdays	• Longer meeting time • Freedom from distractions	• Interferes with personal/family time
Summer	• Longer meeting time • Freedom from distractions	• Difficult to keep others informed and to solicit input
Inservice days	• Longer meeting time • Freedom from distractions	• May interfere with school/district staff development efforts • Length of time between meetings
Released time	• Longer meeting time • Freedom from distractions	• Teachers not with students • Need to prepare substitute plans
Electronic	• Increases flexibility • Saves time	• Not as easy to iron out differences of opinion

In one district we know of, the superintendent made a commitment to do all curriculum work on release time once a month for a full school day. Since a shortage of substitute teachers threatened to make this impossible, free two-day substitute teacher training workshops were offered for potential substitutes, and the school board agreed to pay substitutes who had completed the workshop an extra $2.00 on each day they subbed. Teachers were excited at first that they would not have to devote after-school time to curriculum meetings, but over time, committee members became increasingly concerned about the amount of time they were spending away from their classrooms. They opted to meet after school instead, and the superintendent agreed to pay them a percentage of the money that would have been paid to a substitute teacher, the percentage based on the length of the meeting.

There is no perfect answer to the question of meeting times. It is worth seeking input from potential committee members about their preferences regarding meeting days and times before making a final decision. Worksheet 3.4 can be used for this purpose.

You'll also want to select the meeting place with care. It can be excellent for committee morale to meet off-site in a restaurant or hotel conference room, for example, if one is located close enough to the district to be practical and if funds are available for this purpose. However, access to a photocopying machine and computers is critical to the committee process, and this need usually necessitates holding meetings in a school or the central office conference room.

Additional factors merit consideration in your selection of a meeting site. Having a large table or tables at which to work is far preferable to working at student desks, even if these can be put in a circle. Committee meetings are work sessions, and the large amount of paper generated throughout the process and the need to refer to print resources means that committee members need room to spread out. A room with windows is far less oppressive than one without, and comfortable chairs are a must, particularly for lengthy meetings.

NOTIFYING COMMITTEE MEMBERS

Once the committee's charge is clear and membership on the committee is set, a decision about the chairperson has been made, the dates and times for at least the first few meetings have been determined, and a site has been identified, committee members need to be notified. A letter containing this information should be sent to each committee member as far in advance of the first meeting as possible. Worksheet 3.5 can be used to create the rough draft of this letter and list, which can then be typed and distributed.

BUDGETING FOR CURRICULUM DEVELOPMENT

Curriculum development does cost money, though the total amount need not be exorbitant. A realistic budget, presented at the planning stage, can prevent problems later. Preparation in advance of such a budget also helps to ensure that the resources needed by the curriculum committee will be available, and that committee members won't become frustrated by perceived roadblocks to their process.

Several types of resources are particularly important to the curriculum development process. One that is often overlooked is the need for clerical support for the work of the committee. Curriculum committees are typically made up mostly of teachers, and no teachers we know have secretarial support. Teachers on committees should spend their time and energy on the professional aspects of curriculum development, not on typing meeting minutes or retyping curriculum drafts. It should be made clear from the start who is going to provide clerical support for the committee.

Curriculum development cannot take place in a vacuum. Committee members need access to outside experts, either through bringing in consultants or by attending related state, regional, or national conferences themselves. In fact, attendance at conferences serves a dual purpose: providing an incentive for participation on the committee and promoting committee consideration of recent research and best practices.

A budget needs to be created to ensure that the needed resources will be available. Use Worksheet 3.6 to create your budget for the curriculum development process.

WORKSHEET 3.4   Committee Member Survey: Preferred Meeting Days and Times

To: Members of the _____ Curriculum Development Committee

From:

Date:

Re: Determination of committee meeting times

Please complete the following brief questionnaire and return to me at _____ no later than_____. Thank you.

1. For each of the potential meeting times listed below, please circle the letter that best corresponds to your preference. (H = High, M = Medium, L = Low)

1½ hours weekly after school	H	M	L
3 hours every other week after school	H	M	L
1½ hours weekly in the evening	H	M	L
3 hours weekly in the evening	H	M	L
Half-day released time once a month	H	M	L
Whole day released time once a month	H	M	L
Saturday mornings once a month	H	M	L
Saturday afternoons once a month	H	M	L
All day Saturday once a month	H	M	L
A 3- to 5-day block in the summer	H	M	L
Inservice days	H	M	L
Other: _____	H	M	L

2. If some or all meetings were to take place in the afternoons after school, on which days would you be able to participate? Please circle any days that apply.

Monday   Tuesday   Wednesday   Thursday   Friday

3. Additional comments:

WORKSHEET 3.5 **Committee Member Notification**

To: Members of the _____ Curriculum Development Committee

From:

Date:

Re: Announcement of first committee meeting

Thank you for agreeing to serve on the _____ Curriculum Development Committee. Our first meeting will take place on _____ at _____ in _____.

The members of the committee are:

_____ has agreed to serve as committee chairperson.

WORKSHEET 3.6 Budget for Curriculum Committee Work

For each category, indicate the amount of money that needs to be budgeted for the work of the committee.

Curriculum Committee: _____

Category

1.0 Salaries

    1.1 Teacher

    1.2 Administrator

    1.3 Secretarial

    1.4 Paraprofessional

    1.5 Substitutes

    1.6 Other

2.0 Benefits

3.0 Staff Development

    3.1 Conferences

    3.2 Visitations

    3.3 Courses

    3.4 Workshops

    3.5 Books/Materials

4.0 Consultants

5.0 Other Expenses

    5.1 Copying/Printing

    5.2 Postage

    5.3 Computer Time

    5.4 Supplies

    5.5 Miscellaneous

6.0 Total Expenses

4

Group Dynamics

A Guide for the Committee Chair

Running committee meetings requires the committee chair to facilitate group dynamics and to move the committee efficiently through the process of completing the task at hand. The approaches and tools presented in this chapter are designed to enhance your ability to serve in this role and to support you in your four critical tasks—facilitating meetings, dealing with problem situations, communicating about the work of the committee, and soliciting input and feedback for the work of the committee.

ESTABLISHING GROUND RULES FOR MEETINGS

Ground rules for meetings are principles that guide the ways in which committee members do their work together. Identifying and agreeing to ground rules at the outset helps to establish an efficient approach to getting the job done and to create a pleasant working environment in which differences of opinion can be resolved.

From our experience, we recommend the following committee ground rules, and we present the rationale for each. As a committee, discuss each ground rule, make any revisions you wish, and then adopt them. Once adopted, the ground rules will guide your work together as a committee, and it is important that the chairperson of the committee both model and monitor adherence to the ground rules.

Ground Rule 1. All meetings will begin and end on time.

Meetings that begin and end on time are more productive than those that do not. When meetings begin late, participants soon learn that arriving on time is not important. Participants then tend to arrive later and later, and productive meeting time is lost. Those who arrive on time become annoyed about having to wait to start. When meetings end late, participants become resentful as child care arrangements and other obligations are interfered with.

Ground Rule 2. A 10-minute break will be taken every hour and a half during lengthy committee meetings.

Committee meetings typically involve intense interactions and hard work. Taking a short break every hour and a half allows participants to catch their breath and come back to the task refreshed.

Ground Rule 3. In order to promote efficiency, all members will prepare for meetings by reading background material and by other means, as appropriate.

Preparation is required for most meetings. There may be articles to read, drafts to review, or input to solicit. When members do not carry through on these assignments on time, the work of the entire committee is slowed. Making a joint commitment to come to meetings prepared helps to ensure that committee members will actually do so.

Ground Rule 4. Side conversations should not occur during committee meetings, except as appropriate for small-group discussion of agenda items.

Many of us have a tendency when an idea pops into our head to immediately share it with the person sitting next to us. Unfortunately, this tendency prevents sharing the idea with the entire committee for consideration, and it keeps those who are talking together on the side from participating in and contributing to the task at hand. Adopting this ground rule makes it much easier for the committee chair or committee members to ask those involved to stop talking or to share their point with the group—without offending anyone.

Ground Rule 5. The level of trust will be such that statements and differences expressed within meetings will not be carried beyond the walls of the meeting room.

Differences of opinion are bound to arise during the curriculum process. Such conflicts stand the best chance of being resolved if all participants feel free to honestly state their opinions on a given topic. Such open discussion is enhanced when all involved know that no one is going to go back to the teachers' room and say something like, "You won't believe what Jane said in the meeting yesterday!"

Ground Rule 6. All committee members will serve as representatives of their respective constituencies (school, administrative team, community, etc.).

Each committee member serves not only as an individual but also as a representative of some other group—a school, a grade level, a community group, an administrative team, and so forth. When decisions are being made, it is the responsibility of committee members to be sure that the points of view of all members of the group they represent are made known.

Ground Rule 7. When a difference of opinion exists about a particular issue, every effort will be made to reach a decision by consensus. When consensus cannot be reached in what is deemed by the chairperson to be a reasonable amount of time, the decision will be made by a two-thirds majority vote of those present at the meeting.

The strongest decisions are those reached through consensus—mutual agreement of those involved. While reaching consensus often takes longer than taking a vote, the process that leads up to it usually produces new ideas and improved solutions to problems. At times, however, an issue is not important enough to warrant a lengthy process. When a group is not able to reach consensus and when the issue involved is not a highly emotional one, simply voting on the matter and moving on to the next task may be the best approach.

In cases when a vote is taken, a two-thirds majority vote of those in attendance at the meeting should be required to ensure that there is ample support for the position the committee will take. Less than a two-thirds majority suggests that a real split exists on the issue, both within the committee and probably within the district as well. In such cases further discussion and alternative proposals are needed.

Any decisions, whether reached by consensus or vote, should be made by those in attendance at the meeting at which the decision is required. This promotes attendance at meetings and allows the committee to get on with its work even if some members are absent.

Ground Rule 8. All committee members will support the final product.

The committee process is one of discussion and compromise leading to a final product. It is helpful if all committee members know from the start that they will work together in the end to support and promote the work of the committee, no matter what differences of opinion may have arisen along the way.

Ground Rule 9. Committee members will rotate the responsibility for taking meeting minutes at each meeting. The committee chair will be responsible for seeing that minutes are typed and distributed to all members and all schools.

Meeting minutes are an important record of the decisions made by a committee. It is very difficult for a committee chair to run a meeting and take minutes at the same time. Rotating responsibility for the taking of minutes ensures that no one committee member is expected to take on a disproportionate amount of responsibility for this task. Since teachers and community members often do not have access to secretarial support, it makes the most sense for the committee chair to see to it that minutes are typed and distributed.

Ground Rule 10. Staff members in all schools will be informed of the activities of the committee on a regular basis. This effort will include (but will not be limited to) the posting of all meeting minutes in each school building.

If the committee process is to be a truly representative one, those who will be expected to implement the curriculum must have access to its development at all stages of the process. One way to accomplish this purpose is to post meeting minutes in all schools and to note that input and feedback are desired.

Worksheet 4.1 is a ground rules draft for the committee to review, revise, and adopt.

WORKSHEET 4.1   Ground Rules Draft

Below is a draft of ground rules for committee meetings. Please read over this draft and note any additions, revisions, or deletions you think we should make before our committee adopts the ground rules.

1. All meetings will begin and end on time.

2. A 10-minute break will be taken every hour and a half during lengthy committee meetings.

3. In order to promote efficiency, all members will prepare for meetings by reading background material and by other means, as appropriate.

4. Side conversations will not occur during committee meetings, except as appropriate for small-group discussion of agenda items.

5. The level of trust will be such that statements and differences expressed within meetings will not be carried beyond the walls of the meeting room.

6. All committee members will serve as representatives of their respective constituencies.

7. When a difference of opinion exists about a particular issue, every effort will be made to reach a decision by consensus. When consensus cannot be reached in what is deemed by the chairperson to be a reasonable amount of time, the decision will be made by a two-thirds majority vote of those present at the meeting.

8. All committee members will support the final product.

9. Committee members will rotate the responsibility for taking minutes at each meeting. The committee chair will be responsible for seeing that minutes are typed and distributed to all members and all schools.

10. Staff members in all schools will be informed of the activities of the committee on a regular basis. This effort will include (but not be limited to) the timely posting of all meeting minutes in each school building.

Adopted: _____

Date: _____

Committee member signatures:

CREATING A COMMITTEE DATABASE

It is worthwhile to establish at the start a database of information about members of the committee. Doing so provides a sense of the background and areas of expertise of committee members and helps determine in what areas the committee may need professional development during the process of creating the K–12 curriculum guidelines. Worksheet 4.2 can be used to gather information from committee members for the database.

MEETING MINUTES

Meeting minutes serve as a record of the work and decisions of the committee. Meeting minutes should *not* be a running record of who said what about which issues. They need not be lengthy, but they should accurately represent what has transpired during a meeting.

Meeting minutes should include the following:

- The date of the meeting
- A list of committee members present and absent at each meeting
- A concise overview of the meeting
- A list of agreements reached by committee members
- Any drafts or revisions ready for reaction
- The date, time, and place of the next meeting
- The agenda for the next meeting
- A request for input and feedback from all teachers and administrators in the district

Worksheet 4.3 can be duplicated and used to record the minutes of each meeting.

MEETING FACILITATION

Meeting facilitation requires specific skills on the part of the committee chairperson, including the following:

- Timing interactions
- Promoting teamwork
- Mediating conflicts
- Dealing with problem situations

TIMING INTERACTIONS

Timing is a critical factor in the work of any committee. Members become frustrated when discussions bog down; they also tend to get angry if discussion is cut off prematurely. Too much time on any one task results in an overall process that takes much longer than it needs to; too little time results in a lower quality product and less support of the product from committee members during the implementation phase. Clearly, timing is a tricky issue.

In general, you will find

- The more disagreement there is about an issue, the more time needs to be spent on the issue.
- The more complex the issue, the more time needs to be spent on the issue.
- Logistical issues take less time than philosophical ones.

WORKSHEET 4.2 Committee Database Sheet

Please complete this worksheet and bring it with you to the next committee meeting. Please attach one copy of any article you reference in the final section of this worksheet.

Name: _____

Related Teaching Experience

School	Grades/Subjects	Dates

_____

_____

_____

_____

Related Courses and Workshops

Title	Location	Dates	Credits

_____

_____

_____

_____

_____

Books and Articles Recommended for Committee Use

_____

_____

_____

_____

WORKSHEET 4.3 Meeting Minutes Template

Committee   Meeting Date

Members Present

Members Absent

Meeting Overview

Agreements Reached

Drafts or Revisions (attach separate sheet if necessary)

Date/Times/Place of Next Meeting

Agenda for Next Meeting

To Teachers and Administrators: We need your feedback! Please contact your committee representative to share your comments.

PROMOTING TEAMWORK

Teamwork connotes collaboration for a common purpose—in this case, production of the curriculum guidelines. The role of the chair in building teamwork cannot be overstated. We recommend the following tactics:

- Establish trust.
  - ○ Listen objectively to suggestions and complaints.
  - ○ Adhere to ground rules adopted by the committee.
  - ○ Demonstrate fairness in assignment of tasks.
  - ○ Carry your own weight as a committee member; that is, take on tasks beyond merely chairing committee meetings.
- Acknowledge and use members' strengths.
  - ○ Never do something yourself a committee member can do better.
  - ○ Refer frequently to specific examples of individual committee members' contributions to the task.
- Limit the number of tasks to be completed by individuals.
  - ○ Create new "pairings" across grade levels, between schools, and so forth.
  - ○ Share your rationale for asking particular committee members to carry out specific tasks. Reference concrete examples that qualify the individuals you have chosen.
  - ○ Use subcommittees to draft scope-and-sequence sections. (Be sure to clarify, though, that the authority of the subcommittee is limited and that only the full committee can make final decisions.)
- Allow time for committee members to socialize and have fun together.

MEDIATING CONFLICT

Conflict can and should be a positive force in the committee process. It is the role of the chair to create a safe environment in which conflicts can be worked out, to bring to the surface conflicts that exist between members and make certain these are explored and resolved, and to help the committee reflect on its mutual success in working through conflict situations. Some specific strategies are particularly useful:

1. Early in the process of development, tell committee members that conflict and differences of opinion are bound to arise in the group and that this is both expected and OK. Acknowledge that many of us have learned from an early age to avoid conflict situations, but that this is detrimental to the creative process.

2. Don't take the silence of a committee member to mean agreement with a decision that is about to be made. Particularly when an issue is an emotional or difficult one, go around the table and ask each committee member to state an opinion on the topic under discussion before a final decision is made.

3. Mention the successes the committee has had in working through conflict situations. Note the creative solutions that have evolved because the committee took time to look at and work through differences of opinion.

4. Mediate conflict situations by moderating the ensuing discussion, much as one would a debate. Set rules for the discussion, such as that only one person at a time will speak, personal remarks are not allowed, and the like.

DEALING WITH PROBLEM SITUATIONS

Particular kinds of problem situations are common to the curriculum process. It is useful to give some thought to these before you actually encounter them. Worksheet 4.4 presents case studies based on actual problem situations we have encountered.

Important—Complete Worksheet 4.4 <u>before</u> reading the next section, Strategies for Dealing with Problem Situations.

STRATEGIES FOR DEALING WITH PROBLEM SITUATIONS

The appropriate response to problem situations varies depending on the context and the individuals involved. We offer the following strategies not as *the* answer but as approaches we have used that have usually worked for us.

1. "I don't like it."

- Ask Bill what it is *specifically* that he doesn't like.
- Ask Bill to recommend an alternative.
- Tell Bill the committee has spent a considerable amount of time on the philosophy and, unless he can be more specific, it really does seem time to send out the draft for reaction and input.
- Say to Bill, "You don't like this draft and you're not sure why. Let's send it out for input and reaction. Maybe others who read this with new eyes will identify the problem and offer a solution."

2. "We've been here before."

- Explain that in the past there may have been little or no follow-up on the curriculum development process. Review the district's current curriculum model. Emphasize the relationship between curriculum development, implementation, and assessment and the district's commitment to all three components of the process.
- Ask committee members to make a commitment to seeing that the document does not become a "shelf" document.
- Take time to have the committee brainstorm specific strategies to ensure that there is follow-through when the guidelines are complete.

3. "But I've always taught Dinosaurs."

- Acknowledge that you understand that Bob has reason to be upset.
- Explain that the decision about where particular topics will be taught at which grade level(s) needs to be based on what is best for students, not only on teacher preference.
- Make sure that another topic that Bob likes to teach is placed at his grade level.

4. "There is one right way."

- Use processes that prevent domination, such as cooperative groups and calling on all committee members in turn during a discussion.
- Meet with George and Jean individually. Talk with them about the needs of the group and what needs to be done.

5. "I don't get it."

- Have all committee members meet in pairs to list "What we know about _____."
- Assign Elizabeth relatively simple tasks.
- Say to Elizabeth, "Let's get together after the meeting to go over that."
- Pair Elizabeth with a stronger committee member for completion of tasks.

(Text continues on page 66)

WORKSHEET 4.4 Case Studies: Problem Situations

Below is a series of mini case studies representing difficult situations we have encountered in our own work. Following each, briefly note what you would do if you were confronted with each of these problems. When you have finished, check your solutions against those presented on pages 63 and 66.

1. "I don't like it."

Just when everything is going along smoothly—the committee is on the verge of adopting the philosophy statement after much discussion and compromise, for example—Bill says, "I don't like it." This statement seems to come from out of the blue, and other committee members are clearly stunned. They turn to you for a response. What do you do?

_____

_____

_____

2. "We've been here before."

At the first committee meeting, introductions have been completed and ground rules have been adopted. You're ready to start the process of developing reviewing the standards and performance indicators to be included in the document when Janet says, "Haven't we been here before? I mean, I was on a committee like this 15 years ago and we spent months developing the curriculum. When we finished, I never heard about it again. I mean, why bother? What's the point of all this work?" What do you do?

_____

_____

_____

3. "But I've always taught Dinosaurs."

Through the process of curriculum mapping, the committee has discovered that the topic of dinosaurs is taught in kindergarten, first, second, third, and fourth grades. In developing the scope-and-sequence section of the document, the committee has decided that this much overlap on one topic is undesirable and is leaning toward designating second grade as the grade level in which this topic will be used as a focus for interdisciplinary curriculum. Betty, a second-grade teacher, is clearly pleased with this decision, but Bob, a third-grade teacher, folds his arms across his chest, leans back in his chair, looks you straight in the eye, and says, "I've been teaching Dinosaurs for 10 years. The district has spent more than $2,000 on materials I use for this unit, and I've spent at least $500 of my own money on posters and cassette tapes to go along with the unit. Do you mean to tell me I won't be able to use those materials any more? What do you think the taxpayers would have to say about that?" What do you do?

_____

_____

_____

4. "There is one right way."

George has taught courses related to this area of the curriculum, and he has "all the answers." There is one right way, and that anyone with any sense should agree with him is something he makes clear in his every word and deed in committee meetings. The same could be said of Jean, another committee member, but her "one right way" is directly opposed to George's. These two dominate committee discussions with their disagreements, and each seems more interested in getting the greatest number of committee members to agree with him or her than in getting the job done. What do you do?

_____

_____

_____

5. "I don't get it."

Elizabeth has been in the district for 10 years, and she is highly regarded by parents and colleagues for her warm and caring nature and her sensitivity to children. She is not, however, very bright. Her standard response to almost anything that comes up in the committee's discussions is, "I don't get it." Committee members are becoming increasingly irritated with the need to stop and explain things to her. What do you do?

_____
_____
_____

6. "Why reinvent the wheel?"

John arrives at the first committee meeting with a copy of the neighboring district's document for the curriculum area you're about to develop. He says, "They just spent two years putting this document together, and it looks pretty good to me. They teach the same standards and grade level expectations we do. Why reinvent the wheel? Why don't we just adopt this one and go home?" What do you do?

_____
_____
_____

7. "Does anyone have a thesaurus?"

The committee is processing curriculum guidelines and is working to decide which ideas are most important to incorporate. Laura pipes up, "Does anyone have a thesaurus? The verb in this sentence just isn't right, and we've already used it twice on this page. Also, I think we have some real problems here with punctuation. We better fix this." What do you do?

_____
_____
_____

8. "The thing about research is . . ."

You've copied and distributed to all committee members the articles that were recommended on their data sheets. You are about to conduct a group listing of key points from the research when David states unequivocally, "Research is useless. You can make it say anything you want it to say." Mary disagrees, saying, "We really need to consider the research, but there aren't enough articles here. There's a lot more out there, and we ought to read it all." What do you do?

_____
_____
_____

9. "I can't stand her."

Two members of the committee, Gwen and Lorraine, have a long-standing animosity toward one another. Both are important participants on the committee because of their expertise and their standing in the district. After the second meeting, Gwen comes to your office in tears and says she needs to resign from the committee. She blurts out, "I can't work with Lorraine. I just can't stand her." What do you do?

_____
_____
_____

After responding to each of the problem situations above, refer to pages 63 and 66 for suggested strategies to use in dealing with them.

6. "Why reinvent the wheel?"

- Explain the importance of process over product—that if the curriculum is going to become "real" within the district, district teachers need to be involved in developing it.
- Explain that wholesale adoption of an already published curriculum can be appropriate at times when there is little controversy in the district about that area of the curriculum and when there will be relatively little impact on students, but that this isn't one of those times.
- You might quote Bruce Joyce, who reportedly has said, "We need to reinvent the wheel from time to time not because we need more wheels, but because we need more inventors."

7. "Does anyone have a thesaurus?"

- Assure Laura that the committee will ultimately edit the guidelines for proper word choice and punctuation. Explain that first it is important for the committee to agree on the ideas it wishes to include in the guidelines.
- Ask Laura if, when the guidelines are completed, she would do the final edit on them.
- Ask Laura to go to the library to get a thesaurus and to come back with a proposal.

8. "The thing about research is . . ."

- Explain to David that when conflicting research findings are found, the philosophy developed by the committee can be used to decide which findings to use.
- Agree that all research is not created equal and point out that the hallmark of a professional is the ability to read the literature of the profession critically.
- Say to Mary, "The reality is, we can't read everything. We need to be selective. However, if there's something important you think we've missed, bring it to the table."
- Make Mary the chair of the subcommittee that is charged to review and synthesize for the entire committee related literature.

9. "I can't stand her."

- Sit Gwen and Lorraine down together and state explicitly that they have got to work together and they can't behave like this anymore. This committee assignment is their professional responsibility, and they need to set personal issues aside.

COMMUNICATING PROGRESS AND SOLICITING INPUT AND FEEDBACK

As it goes about its work, a curriculum committee represents the entire district. It is important, therefore, that all in the district—teachers, administrators, community members, students—know what it is the committee is charged to do and have the opportunity to provide input and feedback throughout the process. While all committee members should be involved in this process, it is the committee chair who is responsible for overseeing the process and ensuring that there is ample communication between the committee and the constituencies within the district it represents.

In general, you will find

- The more controversial the history of this area of curriculum in the district, the more communication there needs to be.
- The larger the district, the more varied the forms of communication that need to be used.
- The longer it has been since an area of the curriculum was addressed, the more communication there needs to be about the goals of the curriculum process.

Use Worksheet 4.5 to determine which approaches to communication you will use and who is responsible for each. Worksheet 4.6 can be used to gather directed feedback on committee drafts throughout the curriculum development process.

Chapter 5, Developing the K–12 Curriculum Guidelines, focuses on the substance of the work the committee is charged to do.

WORKSHEET 4.5 Communication Checklist

Numerous communication tools and processes can be used to solicit input and feedback about curriculum processes and products from a variety of audiences. Use the checklist below to determine which approaches will be used and who is responsible for each.

Approach   *Person(s) Responsible*

❑   Letter to all staff members describing the process
    and timeline for developing this curriculum area

❑   Letter to community members describing the
    process and timeline for developing this curriculum
    area

❑   Minutes posted regularly in each school building

❑   Staff meeting presentation(s) and response sheet

❑   School board presentation(s) and response sheet

❑   Administrative team presentation(s) and response
    sheet

❑   Community forum for gathering input

❑   Focused interviews with influential individuals in the
    schools and community

❑   Other: _____

WORKSHEET 4.6 Response Sheet

The _____ Curriculum Development Committee needs your input. Attached is a draft of our work to date. Please take a few minutes to read over the draft and complete the sheet below. Return this sheet to _____ by _____. Thank you.

What do you like about this draft?

What would you like to see us add?

What would you like to see us remove?

Other comments:

5

Developing the K–12 Curriculum Guidelines

The process presented in this chapter is designed to support a productive, worthwhile experience that will ultimately lead to the production of high-quality K–12 curriculum guidelines. The K–12 curriculum guidelines are an overview and general plan for a curriculum area. The guidelines should include

- Purpose statement
- Curriculum goals
- Scope and sequence of standards-based performance objectives and grade-level expectations
- Instructional guidelines
- Needs and recommendations
- Program evaluation statement

THE PURPOSE STATEMENT

The *purpose statement* is a clear, brief statement of the purpose and nature of the curriculum for a particular area of study. It is consistent with the district's vision statement (see Chapter 1), but it is more specific in that it justifies the inclusion of the given curriculum area in the overall district curriculum. When completed, the purpose statement serves as an important basis for making decisions about what should and what should not be included in the remaining sections of the K–12 curriculum guidelines.

The purpose statement

- Defines the curriculum area to be addressed by the guidelines
- States the district's purposes for having the students learn the subject
- Articulates the district's position on how students best learn the concepts, content, and skills of that curriculum area

Figure 5.1 shows a sample curriculum purpose statement, while Figure 5.2 describes the process that can be used to develop the purpose statement for the curriculum guidelines. Worksheets 5.1 and 5.2 can be used to draft the purpose statement.

Figure 5.1 Sample Curriculum Purpose Statement

Sample Curriculum Purpose Statement: Language Arts

The language arts curriculum guidelines apply to the areas of reading, writing, listening, and speaking. These four areas require and promote complex thinking, are interdependent across all content areas, and are equally important in developing literacy.

The purpose of learning language arts is to enable students to communicate for personal fulfillment, for success in work, and participation in a democratic society and the global community.

Students learn best when they use their language—reading, writing, listening, and speaking—in authentic activities appropriate for their developmental stages and different learning styles.

From the Addison Northeast Supervisory Union K–12 Curriculum Guidelines for Language Arts Used with permission.

Figure 5.2 How to Develop a Curriculum Purpose Statement

The process described below is designed to produce a purpose statement that reflects the contributions of all committee members. The committee chairperson can take the committee through the following steps.

1. Review with the committee what a curriculum purpose statement is.

2. Provide each committee member with a copy of Worksheet 5.1, the Curriculum Purpose Development Worksheet.

3. Ask committee members to work alone to complete each section of the worksheet.

4. When all committee members have finished writing, ask them to take turns reading their responses for the first open-ended statement. Tell them that the plan is to listen for common themes and that discussion will take place after all committee members have had an opportunity to read their responses.

5. When all committee members have read their responses for the first statement, ask the group, "Are there any observations or reactions?"

6. Note areas of agreement and disagreement during the discussion that follows.

7. Summarize areas of agreement and ask committee members if your summary is accurate. If all committee members agree that the summary is accurate, move on to Step 8. If any committee member does not accept the summary, revise your summary to the satisfaction of all participants.

8. Summarize areas of disagreement, if any.

9. Lead committee members in a discussion through which areas of disagreement are clarified and resolved, compromise is reached, or a decision is made to omit an area of disagreement from the philosophy statement.

10. Repeat Steps 4 through 8 for the second and then the third open-ended statement from Worksheet 5.1, the Curriculum Purpose Development Worksheet.

11. When all differences have been resolved and all areas of agreement are clarified, break the committee into three subcommittees for the purpose of drafting a philosophy statement.

12. Cut apart the three sections from each committee member's worksheet and give all #1 responses to one group, #2 to another group, and #3 to the third group.

---

13. Tell all subcommittees that their task is to draft a statement representing the areas of agreement discussed by the full committee.

14. When all three subcommittees have completed their work, paste the three drafts together in order and make enough copies for all committee members.

15. Work with the whole committee to edit and refine this draft of the curriculum purpose statement.

16. Provide committee members with sample curriculum purpose statements from other school districts. Ask them to read these statements and consider whether anything has been left out of their own statement. If necessary, revise the committee's curriculum purpose statement draft.

17. Seek full committee approval of the final draft of the curriculum purpose statement.

18. Share the curriculum purpose statement with all staff members and administrators in the district and solicit reactions and input.

19. Revise the curriculum purpose statement, if necessary.

20. Seek full committee approval of the final curriculum purpose statement.

CURRICULUM GOALS

Curriculum goals are goals for students, statements of the expected results of the curriculum. They state the broad areas of concepts, skills, knowledge, and attitudes it is hoped that students will know and exhibit as a result of completing the K–12 program. Most curriculum documents contain from 3 to 12 curriculum goals. The following are examples of curriculum goals:

- Students will communicate orally, with ease, in a variety of settings.
- Students will use mathematics to solve problems in the everyday world.
- Students will act to ensure and protect a healthy environment for generations to come.

Statements such as "Students will be engaged in a multidisciplinary approach to the study of science" are not learning goals because they are not statements of results. Instead, they are statements of instructional guidelines, the instructional approaches necessary to help students achieve curriculum goals.

The process for developing curriculum goals is described in Figure 5.3. Worksheets 5.3 and 5.4 can be used to develop your curriculum goals.

THE SCOPE AND SEQUENCE OF OBJECTIVES

The scope and sequence of objectives specifies the concepts, skills, and content that students need to be able to understand, do, and know in order to attain the stated curriculum goals. *Scope* refers to what is "covered" in the curriculum, and it is usually represented in the form of strands or categories that are used to organize and present the expectations sequenced in the guidelines. *Sequence* establishes the order in which specific concepts, skills, and content are expected to be learned or taught. These expectations are expressed in the form of objectives, written operational statements that show expectations for a particular grade level (K, 1, 2, etc.) or grade-level block (i.e., K–3, 4–6, 7–8, 9–12).

In the case of a standards-based scope and sequence, the objectives can usually be drawn directly from the performance indicators, benchmarks, or grade-level expectations from state standards documents and other sets of recommendations, such as those from national professional organizations such as the National Council of Teachers of Mathematics (NCTM). When standards documents were first developed, some districts would simply adopt state documents as the local curriculum. While

WORKSHEET 5.1 Curriculum Purpose Development Worksheet

Please write responses to the following statements.

1. _____ is/consists of _____

                                   (curriculum area)

_____

_____

_____

_____

_____

_____

2. The purpose of learning _____ concepts, skills, and content is

                                   (curriculum area)

_____

_____

_____

_____

_____

_____

_____

3. Students best learn _____ concepts, skills, and

                                   (curriculum area)

    content when/by _____

_____

_____

_____

_____

_____

_____

WORKSHEET 5.2   Curriculum Purpose Statement—Final Draft

In the space below, write the final draft of the curriculum purpose statement approved by the curriculum development committee for inclusion in the K–12 guidelines.

Figure 5.3 How to Develop Curriculum Goals

The committee chairperson should take the committee through the following steps:

1. Review with all committee members what curriculum goals are.

2. Provide each committee member with a copy of Worksheet 5.3, the Goals Development Worksheet.

3. Ask committee members to use the worksheet to brainstorm possible goals for the curriculum area.

4. When committee members finish writing, ask them to share possible goal statements from their brainstormed lists. Use a felt-tip marker to record these on large chart paper.

5. Lead the committee in a discussion of the resulting list. Add, delete, and revise as necessary to complete a first draft of the committee's list of curriculum goals. (Note: Since all goals are equally important, they are not usually presented in any particular order of priority. It is appropriate, however, to cluster goals that are related to one another.)

6. Provide committee members with sample copies of goals for the same curriculum area from other school districts. Ask committee members to read through these goals and consider whether anything they value has been left off their own list.

7. Revise goals list, if necessary.

8. Ask committee members to reread the philosophy statement they drafted earlier. Are all goals consistent with the purpose statement?

9. Revise the goals list and purpose, if necessary.

10. Seek full committee approval of the current list of curriculum goals.

11. Share the curriculum goals with staff members and administrators in the district and solicit reactions and input.

12. Revise the goals list, if necessary.

13. Seek full committee approval of the final list of curriculum goals.

this approach established the scope of the curriculum, it did little or nothing to establish the sequence. Teachers were left with no direction as to when particular objectives should be taught and assessed in the classroom. Districts with which we work typically organize the scope-and-sequence document by quarter or by month. Figure 5.4 below is adapted from the scope and sequence for first quarter writing for 10th grade in the Enlarged City School District of Middletown.

Many scope-and-sequence documents provide, in addition to the standards-based objectives, guidance for the pacing of the objectives, as well as recommendations and examples of instructional materials and assessments that can be used to effectively teach and assess the objectives. The example of a scope-and-sequence document shown in Figure 5.4 provides in one easy-to-access location the objectives that need to be taught and assessed during the quarter, the materials that can be used to teach and assess them, and the assessments that can be used to give students feedback about their learning. This particular example also includes reference to a common benchmark assessment that is used by all teachers of the course to gauge the extent to which the students have attained the objectives or performance indicators.

The next example, Figure 5.5, shows the scope-and-sequence document in the Elmira City School District for second grade English language arts (ELA) for the month of September. The scope and sequence for each month are presented on two pages that face each other. The objectives or performance indicators are presented on the left-hand side of the page. The "I can" statements are performance indicators that are taught and assessed each month, not just in September. They have been translated into "I can" statements that students themselves can focus on and assess as to their strengths and what they next need to learn.

WORKSHEET 5.3 Goals Development

In the space below, brainstorm a list of results that you hope the entire K–12 program for this curriculum area will achieve. What will students know? Understand? Feel? Believe? Be able to do?

As a result of the K–12 _____ program in the

(curriculum area)

_____ School District, students will:

(name of district)

WORKSHEET 5.4 Curriculum Goals—Final Draft

In the space below, write the final draft of the goals approved by the curriculum development committee for inclusion in the K–12 guidelines.

Figure 5.4 Sample 10th Grade Scope and Sequence for ELA: Writing

Middletown Scope and Sequence		
Subject Area: ELA: Writing	Quarter: 1	Grade: 10—Holt 4th Course
Standards Key Ideas/Major Understandings/Performance Indicators/Competencies	**Resources (Print, Visual, Technology, Manipulatives)**	**Assessment (Evidence and Scoring Guides)**
Information and understanding 1. Use both primary and secondary sources of information for research 2. Use both primary and secondary sources of information for research 3. Analyze data, facts, and ideas to communicate information 4. Take notes and organize information from written and oral texts, such as lectures and interviews 5. Use a range of organizational strategies (e.g., clustering, webbing, and mapping) to present information 6. Maintain a portfolio that includes informational writing **Literary response and expression** 7. Use resources such as personal experience, knowledge from other content areas, and independent reading to create literary, interpretive, and responsive texts 8. Maintain a portfolio that includes literary, interpretive, and responsive writing **Critical analysis and evaluation** 9. Maintain a writing portfolio that includes writing for critical analysis and evaluation **Social interaction** 10. Share the process of writing with peers and adults; for example, write a condolence note, get-well card, or thank you letter with writing partner(s) 11. Distinguish between the conventions of academic writing and the conventions of e-mail and instant messaging	1. *Lord of the Flies** 2. *The Pearl* 3. *The Strange Case of Jekyll and Hyde* 4. "Monkey's Paw" 5. "The Secret Life of Walter Mitty" 6. Teacher-selected biography or autobiography from text *Minimum of 6 full-length works a year	1. Fictional biography or autobiography 2. Letter designed for specific audiences 3. Paragraph tests 4. Maintain a writing portfolio (submissions Nov. 15, Feb. 15, and May 1) *Quarterly* *1st Benchmark* *"Mini-Research"*

Adapted with permission from the Enlarged City School District of Middletown, NY.

*See Holt Text/2007 NY Edition/Detailed Correlation

Figure 5.5   Example of Second-Grade Scope and Sequence for September

ELA	GRADE 2	SEPTEMBER

Performance Indicators/Competencies

Reading

- ★ I can use what I know about letters, sounds and words to help me figure out words.
- ★ I can read carefully and use what I know about words to fix mistakes.
- ★ I can read with fluency and expression.
- ★ I can connect what I read with my life.
- ★ I can answer questions and solve problems using information.

P-Decode by analogy using **word families (H)**
C-Read and understand directions
C-Identify **main ideas/**supporting details in informational text (with assistance) **(H)**
C-Ask questions when listening to or reading text
V-Develop new vocabulary by studying categories of words(e.g. transportation, sports)
C-Evaluate the content by identifying (with assistance) the **author's purpose,** important/unimportant
   details, whether events, actions, characters, and/or setting are realistic **(H)**

Writing

- ★ I can write about what I know, give information, and tell a story.
- ★ I can write in complete sentences with correct spelling, punctuation, and capitals. (H)
- ★ I can plan my writing in different ways. My writing follows a plan, stays on topic, and has
   important details. (H)

- • Represents all the sounds in a word when spelling independently (phonetic-transitional)
- • State **main idea** and support it with **facts,** with assistance (H)
- • Use resources such as personal experiences to stimulate writing (with assistance)
- • Make judgments about relevant and irrelevant content
- • Correctly spell words that follow the **spelling patterns** of words previously studied (H)
- • Use knowledge of story (B-M-E), problem/solution and story elements (character, setting, plot) to
   interpret stories (with assistance)

Listening

- ★ I can pay attention, ask and answer questions to show I've been listening and follow spoken
   directions.

- • Listens respectfully, without interrupting
- • Attend to a listening activity for a specified period of time

Speaking

- ★ I can speak using complete sentences to share ideas.

- • Use grade level vocabulary to communicate ideas/emotions/experiences for different purposes
- • Take turns in conversation and respond respectfully
- • Use complete sentences with age/content appropriate vocabulary
- • Compare texts and performances to experiences and prior knowledge (with assistance)
- • Take turns speaking in a group/avoid interruptions during conversations

* Top 10 ~ Year Long Performance Indicators

H = Harcourt Skill or Strategy	V = Vocabulary
PA = Phonemic Awareness	F = Fluency
P = Phonics	C = Comprehension

ELA	GRADE 2	SEPTEMBER (cont.)

ASSESSMENTS	RESOURCES

Reading
 	
DIBELS
  -NWF (50)
  -ORF (44)
High frequency words
Ongoing, informal assessments
 	
Writing
 	
Personal narrative writing prompt (portfolio)
Ongoing, informal assessments & conferences utilizing rubrics from 6+1 Traits
 	
Listening
 	
Ongoing, informal assessments
 	
Speaking
 	
Ongoing, informal assessments
	Theme 1: Being Me (Self Discovery)
	
	Mixed Up Chameleon
	Get Up & Go
	Eric Carle trade books and website
	Frog & Toad Are Friends series

SKILLS & STRATEGIES	INTERDISCIPLINARY CONNECTIONS
Reading • -id,-ide • -ame, -ake • -ed endings **Writing** • Responds to literature • Imaginative stories • Personal narratives • Write legibly all uppercase and lowercase manuscript letters	Chameleons

NOTES	KEY TERMS
	Word families/parts Written/oral directions Comprehension Main idea Connections Supporting details Story structure (B,M,E) Facts Decode Setting Questions/questioning Problem/solution Story elements Informational text Author's purpose Vocabulary Background knowledge/schema

Used with permission of the Elmira City School District.

On the second page are found associated skills and strategies from the reading text used in the district, assessments and resources to be used in teaching the objectives, interdisciplinary connections to be pursued that month, and key terms students should learn to use. A place is also provided for teachers to write notes as they use the scope-and-sequence document in their planning.

ORGANIZING THE SCOPE AND SEQUENCE

How should the scope and sequence be organized? The scope and sequence can be organized by grade level (K, 1, 2, etc.), grade range (K–3, 4–6, etc.), age range (6–8, 9–10, etc.), developmental stage (early mature reader, etc.), continuous progress (no discrete benchmarks), or course (English 9, Algebra I, etc.). Each choice of approach to sequencing objectives has potential advantages and disadvantages, which are shown in Figure 5.6.

In standards-based systems we have worked with, the scope and sequence is most typically presented by grade level for the elementary and middle school grades and by course in the high schools. When the scope and sequence is organized by course, it is essential to cross check by course-taking patterns: Do all students have the opportunity to learn all required standards, performance objectives, or grade-level expectations?

HOW TO DEVELOP A SCOPE AND SEQUENCE

The organization of the scope and sequence should reflect the philosophical perspectives of those who will use it as the basis for instruction, and it should respond to the way the schools in your district are organized. Figure 5.7 provides a process for developing your scope and sequence.

Figure 5.6   Approaches to Sequencing Objectives: Advantages and Disadvantages

Advantages	Disadvantages
Grade Level	
• Specifies in advance desired performance for each grade level • Gives clear message to teachers of what they are expected to teach	• Assumes all same-grade students are at the same developmental level
Grade Range/Developmental Level	
• Allows greater chronological span for achieving specified concepts, content, and skills	• Depends on teacher decision making and communication to ensure continuity from year to year
Continuous Progress	
• Lends itself to individualization	• Depends on teacher decision making and communication to ensure continuity from year to year
Course	
• Specifies in advance desired performance for each course • Gives clear message to teachers about each course of what they are expected to teach	• Assumes all students in a particular course are at the same developmental level • Requires articulation of relationship among courses

Figure 5.7   How to Develop the Scope and Sequence

The committee chairperson should take the committee through the following steps:

1. Review with all committee members the definition of the scope and sequence of objectives.

2. Distribute Worksheet 5.5, the Scope and Sequence Decision-Making Worksheet, to all committee members.

3. Decide which strands or categories will provide the basis for organizing the objectives in the curriculum guide. For example, will language arts be divided up as reading, writing, listening, and speaking, or as reading, writing, listening, speaking, library skills, grammar, media, and study skills? Will social studies be categorized as history, sociology, anthropology, psychology, and political science or in some other way? Base these decisions on a review of the committee's purpose statement, on an analysis of current research related to the curriculum area, on awareness of applicable state and federal mandates, and on consideration of categories or strands utilized in curriculum guides from other school districts or from state or national examples of scope and sequence (see Chapter 1).

4. Fill in the strands the committee agrees to use on the Scope and Sequence Decision-Making Worksheet.

5. Decide whether the scope and sequence of objectives will be presented by specific grade levels (K, 1, 2, etc.), by grade-level blocks (i.e., K–3, 4–6, 7–8, 9–12), or by courses. Which organization will be most easily used by teachers as they plan and implement instruction in the classroom?

6. Fill in the grade levels or grade-level blocks the committee agrees to use to develop the scope and sequence of objectives on the Scope and Sequence Decision-Making Worksheet.

7. Provide for all committee members samples of standards-based scope and sequence from the curriculum documents of other school districts (which you have obtained using Worksheet 5.7) and relevant state standards documents. Ask committee members to assess these samples and determine which are most compatible with the purpose and goals established by the committee. If state standards and performance indicators are mandated to be included in the classroom, set up a system to cross-check to see that none are inadvertently left out.

8. Assign subcommittees, either by categories/strands or by grade levels or grade-level blocks, to draft the scope and sequence for the curriculum guidelines. In order to be sure that all committee members understand their task, review with the committee Figure 5.8, the Sample Scope and Sequence Worksheet.

9. Provide copies of Worksheet 5.6, the Scope and Sequence Development Worksheet, for subcommittee members to use in drafting objectives.

10. When all subcommittees have finished drafting the section of the scope and sequence they have been assigned, make copies of all drafts for all committee members.

11. Meet as a full committee to review the various drafts, to revise and edit, and to finalize and approve a complete scope and sequence for the curriculum guide.

12. Ask an outside expert (perhaps a college or university professor or a state department of education consultant for that curriculum area) to critique the scope and sequence of objectives.

13. Share the scope and sequence of objectives with all staff members and administrators in the district and solicit reaction and input.

14. Revise the scope and sequence, if necessary.

15. Seek full committee approval of the final scope and sequence of objectives.

Worksheet 5.5 should be used to record the curriculum development committee's decisions about how the scope and sequence of objectives will be organized.

Once you have decided how your scope and sequence of objectives will be organized, you are ready to articulate the actual objectives for each block of sequence within each strand. Figure 5.8 is a sample worksheet for one block of sequence for one strand of a district's fine arts curriculum. Worksheet 5.6 should be duplicated and used to develop each block of sequence for each strand in your own curriculum document. Worksheet 5.7 can be used to create a letter requesting copies of curriculum documents from other districts.

INSTRUCTIONAL GUIDELINES

Instructional guidelines spell out the kinds of experiences students in all grade levels require in order to attain the goals of the curriculum. While the scope and sequence of objectives specifies what students will learn, instructional guidelines are broad statements about how they will learn it. Instructional guidelines indicate approaches or practices that the curriculum development committee believes will facilitate student learning, and thus they provide the basis for decision making when teachers select materials, programs, or activities to use with students. Instructional guidelines do not mandate specific materials, activities, or programs that must be used by teachers. Instead, it is up to teachers to show how they are implementing instructional guidelines. Figure 5.9 provides sample instructional guidelines that are part of K–5 mathematics curriculum guidelines.

Instructional guidelines may be presented on one page preceding the scope and sequence, or in cases where the guidelines are specific to particular strands within the scope and sequence, the instructional guidelines may be presented at the beginning of each strand. Figure 5.10 outlines the process for developing instructional guidelines. Worksheet 5.8 can be used for developing guidelines. Record your final draft of instructional guidelines on Worksheet 5.9.

Figure 5.8 Sample Scope and Sequence Worksheet

Strand: Studio Art	Grade Level(s): 9–12

Objectives to Be Included

Students will reflect on, interpret, and evaluate works of art, using the language of art criticism. Students will analyze the visual characteristics of the natural and built environment and explain the social, cultural, psychological, and environmental dimensions of the visual arts. Students will compare the ways in which a variety of ideas, themes, and concepts are expressed through the visual arts with the ways they are expressed in other disciplines.

- Use the language of art criticism by reading and discussing critical reviews in newspapers and journals and by writing their own critical responses to works of art (either their own or those of others)
- Explain the visual and other sensory qualities in art and nature and their relation to the social environment
- Analyze and interpret the ways in which political, cultural, social, religious, and psychological concepts and themes have been explored in visual art
- Compare and contrast gradated value with contrasting value; identify complete, symmetrical, and asymmetrical balance within artworks

From the Scope and Sequence for Fine Arts, Enlarged City School District of Middletown, NY. Used with permission.

WORKSHEET 5.5 Scope and Sequence in Decision Making

After reviewing sample curriculum documents from other school districts and from state and national examples, decide as a committee which strands will be used to organize the scope and sequence of objectives. Record below the strands the committee agrees to use.

Strands

Next, decide whether individual grade levels (K, 1, 2, 3, etc.), grade-level blocks (K–2, 3–5, 6–8, etc.), or courses will be used to develop the scope and sequence of objectives. Record the committee's decision below.

WORKSHEET 5.6   Scope and Sequence Development

Strand:

Grade Level(s) or Age Span:

Objectives to Be Included:

WORKSHEET 5.7 Letter Requesting Sample Curriculum Documents

Date:

Dear Curriculum Director:

In the _____ School District, we are currently developing K–12 curriculum guidelines for _____ curriculum area. Your standards-based curriculum for this area has been recommended to us as an example we should review as a part of our own process of development. I am writing to ask for a copy of or a link to your curriculum document.

Please send the curriculum document to me at _____

_____

_____

_____

When we have completed our curriculum development process, we will send you a copy of our document in return. Thank you for your assistance in this important endeavor.

Sincerely,

Figure 5.9 Sample Instructional Guidelines

A high-quality, engaging mathematics classroom shows evidence of the following:

- New York State standards-based curriculum/ECSD monthly webs
- Skills (number sense and operations, algebra, geometry, measurement, statistics and probability) and processes (problem solving, reasoning and proof, representation, communication, connections) taught as directed by NYS and the ECSD
- High expectations for all with appropriate modifications made (i.e., AIS, remediation, enrichment, tutorial)
- Teachers asking questions that promote critical thinking
- Teachers linking new learning with previously learned skills
- Math objectives posted and students able to articulate their learning
- A math block of approximately 60 minutes per day
- Math wall where appropriate grade-level vocabulary is posted and words are defined
- Technology (computers and calculators) available for instructional purposes
- Student engagement using hands-on manipulatives to promote learning for understanding
- Frequent review of previously learned mathematical skills and processes
- Problem solving as a focus of instruction and students seeing connections to real-life applications
- Math centers available for students to review, extend, enrich, and assess understanding
- Mastery of basic math skills for instant recall
- Integration of math into other content areas
- A textbook as one of many resources
- Students seeking the best solution to problems with several options
- Mathematical connections made when students interact with the teacher and with each other through peer partnering, small group activities, math journals, Kagan's cooperative learning tasks, etc.
- Formal and informal assessment techniques used on an ongoing basis; assessments may include but are not limited to open-ended questions, constructed response tasks, selected response items, performance tasks, observations, conversations, journals, portfolios, teacher observations
- Teachers reflecting upon assessment data and making continuous efforts to improve student learning
- Teachers knowing and understanding the math they are teaching and able to differentiate instruction using best practices
- Teachers selecting and using suitable curricular materials, appropriate instructional tools and techniques and engaging and reflecting upon instruction, curriculum and assessment to capture and sustain student's interest and engage students in building math understanding
- Communication and connections made to families to support the learning
- Student work on display
- Organized and well-managed classrooms

Source: A subcommittee of the ECSD's math curriculum committee created this document in Spring 2007. Used with permission of the Elmira City School District.

NEEDS AND RECOMMENDATIONS

Needs and recommendations are statements of what is necessary to make it possible to implement the program. Areas such as budget concerns, required materials, and staff development needs and recommendations are addressed in this section of the curriculum document. Figure 5.11 shows a sample list of needs and recommendations; Figure 5.12 describes a process for developing needs and recommendations for your curriculum guidelines; and Worksheet 5.10 can be used to develop needs and recommendations. Worksheet 5.11 should be used to record the committee's final draft.

Figure 5.10   How to Develop Instructional Guidelines

The committee chairperson should take the committee through the following steps.

1. Review with the committee what instructional guidelines are.

2. Provide each committee member with a copy of Worksheet 5.8, the Instructional Guidelines Worksheet.

3. Ask each member of the committee to consider findings of the review of related educational literature (see Chapter 1) and to work alone to brainstorm a list of possible instructional guidelines the committee should include in the curriculum document.

4. When committee members have finished writing, ask them to share possible instructional guidelines from their brainstormed lists. Use a felt-tip marker to record these on large chart paper.

5. Lead the committee in a discussion of the resulting list. Add, delete, and revise as necessary to complete a first draft of the committee's list of instructional guidelines.

6. Ask the committee members to reread the philosophy statement they drafted earlier. Are the instructional guidelines consistent with the philosophy statement?

7. Revise the instructional guidelines, if necessary.

8. Seek full committee approval of the current draft of the instructional guidelines.

9. Share the instructional guidelines with all staff members and administrators in the district and solicit input and reactions.

10. Revise the instructional guidelines, if necessary.

11. Seek full committee approval of the final list of instructional guidelines.

PROGRAM EVALUATION STATEMENT

The program evaluation statement affirms the district's commitment to evaluate the curriculum in order to answer the following questions: Are students attaining the curriculum goals? Is the curriculum as it is implemented in classrooms throughout the district consistent with the instructional guidelines spelled out in the curriculum document? Have the needs and recommendations articulated by the curriculum committee been addressed? To what extent do students learn the objectives and performance indicators in the scope and sequence?

The program evaluation statement is not a comprehensive plan; rather, it asserts the importance of developing and implementing such a plan (Chapter 10 addresses program evaluation in depth). Figure 5.13 shows a sample program evaluation statement, and Figure 5.14 describes how to develop the statement. Worksheet 5.12 is a proposed program evaluation statement that the committee can complete or revise, and you should use Worksheet 5.13 to record your final program evaluation statement.

When you have completed the K–12 curriculum guidelines, you are ready to publish and celebrate your document.

WORKSHEET 5.8 Instructional Guidelines

In the space below, write a brainstormed list of possible instructional guidelines to be included in the curriculum guide.

In order for students to learn _____ , teachers in all

(curriculum area)

grades need to provide opportunities for them to

WORKSHEET 5.9 Instructional Guidelines—Final Draft

In the space below, record the final draft of instructional guidelines to be included in the curriculum guide.

In order for students to learn _____, teachers in all

(curriculum area)

grades need to provide opportunities for them to

Figure 5.11 Sample Needs and Recommendations—Science

Recommendations of the ANESU Science Curriculum Team
Curriculum Planning and Implementation

- Include specific strategies for implementing the ANESU Science Curriculum Guidelines in each school's action plan including a needs assessment and specific timelines and checkpoints.
- Provide time in each ANESU school for schoolwide or departmentwide implementation of the ANESU Science Curriculum Guidelines.
- Support the teaching of standards-based and research-based curriculum content.
- Promote interdisciplinary approaches to the teaching of science K–12.

Assessment

- Use best practices in assessing student learning.
- Address different learning styles and multiple intelligences in designing standards-based classroom assessments.
- Design standards-based classroom assessments that are performance-based and are embedded, whenever possible, in students' learning activities.
- Publicly display inquiry-based student-designed science investigations annually in all ANESU schools, K–12 (e.g., science fairs, classroom exhibitions, science exhibits at open house). Involve as many students as possible in these annual exhibitions. Use standards-based assessment tools to assess these science projects.

Professional Development

- Offer and encourage quality professional development for all teachers of science, focusing on constructivist and inquiry approaches, standards-based classroom performance assessment, and science content.
- Provide professional development for all supervisors in evaluating best teaching practices in science.
- Establish mentors: elementary/middle/high school teachers who are available to their colleagues K–12 for consultation in the area of science content. Provide incentives (time, $) for teachers to serve as mentors to their colleagues.

Policy

- Develop policy in each school to support the purchase/lease and maintenance of instructional materials necessary to adopt a standards-based science program.

Used with permission of the Addison Northeast Supervisory Union, Vermont.

Figure 5.12 How to Develop Needs and Recommendations

The committee chairperson should take the committee through the following steps.

1. Review with the committee the needs and recommendations.

2. Provide each committee member with a copy of Worksheet 5.10, the Needs and Recommendations Worksheet.

3. Ask each committee member to work alone to brainstorm a list of possible needs and recommendations the committee should include in the curriculum document.

4. When committee members have finished writing, ask them to share possible needs and recommendations from their brainstormed lists. Use a felt-tip marker to record these on large chart paper.

5. Lead the committee in a discussion of the resulting list. Add, delete, and revise as necessary to complete a first draft of the committee's list of needs and recommendations.

6. Seek full committee approval of the current statement of needs and recommendations.

7. Share the needs and recommendations list with all staff members and administrators in the district and solicit input and reactions.

8. Revise the needs and recommendations list, if necessary.

9. Seek full committee approval of the final list of needs and recommendations.

WORKSHEET 5.10 **Needs and Recommendations**

In the space below, write a brainstormed list of possible needs and recommendations to be included in the curriculum guidelines.

In order for the _____, curriculum to be successfully implemented,

WORKSHEET 5.11 Needs and Recommendations—Final Draft

In the space below, record the final draft of the needs and recommendations that the committee agrees should be included in the curriculum guidelines.

In order for the _____ curriculum to be successfully implemented,

(curriculum area)

Figure 5.13   Sample Program Evaluation Statement

The Anywhere, USA, School District is committed to evaluating the district's science curriculum. A variety of techniques will be employed that are best suited to answer the following questions:

- Are students attaining the curriculum goals?
- Is the curriculum as it is implemented consistent with the instructional guidelines spelled out in the curriculum document?
- Have the needs and recommendations articulated by the science curriculum committee been addressed?
- To what extent do students learn the objectives or performance indicators in the scope and sequence?

Program evaluation is not to be confused with teacher evaluation or assessment of individual students. Teachers and administrators will participate in the development of a comprehensive plan for the evaluation of the science program in the Anywhere, USA, School District. When the program evaluation is completed, the results of the assessment will be shared with teachers, administrators, board members, and community members.

Figure 5.14   How to Develop a Program Evaluation Statement

The committee chairperson should take the committee through the following steps.

1. Review with the committee what a program evaluation statement is.

2. Provide each committee member with a copy of Worksheet 5.12, the Proposed Program Evaluation Statement.

3. Read aloud the proposed statement on the worksheet.

4. Ask if anyone would like to suggest revisions to the proposed statement.

5. Make any revisions that are agreed to by the full committee.

6. Ask if anyone would like to make additions to the proposed statement.

7. Make any additions that are agreed to by the full committee.

8. Record the final draft of the statement on Worksheet 5.13.

9. Seek full committee approval of the program evaluation statement.

WORKSHEET 5.12 Proposed Program Evaluation Statement

The _____ School District is committed to evaluating the _____ curriculum. A variety of techniques will be employed that are best suited to help answer the following questions:

- Are students attaining the curriculum goals?

- Is the curriculum as it is implemented in classrooms throughout the district consistent with the instructional guidelines spelled out in the curriculum document?

- Have the needs and recommendations articulated by the curriculum committee been addressed?

- To what extent do students learn the objectives or performance indicators in the scope and sequence?

Program evaluation is not to be confused with teacher evaluation or assessment of individual students. Teachers and administrators will participate in the development of a comprehensive plan for the evaluation of the _____ curriculum in the _____ School District. When the program evaluation is completed, the results of the evaluation will be shared with teachers, administrators, board members, and community members.

WORKSHEET 5.13 Program Evaluation Statement—Final Draft

In the space below, record the final draft of program evaluation statement approved by the curriculum development committee for inclusion in the K–12 curriculum guidelines

6

Publishing and Celebrating the Document

When the work of the curriculum development committee is completed, it is time to publish the guide and celebrate its completion. After all the work the committee has put in, it is worth a little extra time to make sure the document will be attractive, accessible, and easy to use.

PUBLISHING THE DOCUMENT

Since the K–12 curriculum guidelines will be used as the basis for decision making by teachers and administrators throughout the district, the document needs to be as clearly presented and easy to follow as possible. In addition to the actual curriculum guidelines produced, specific items should be included:

- Title page
- Preface
- Table of contents
- List of committee members
- Glossary
- References
- Bibliography
- Appendices

Worksheets for each of these items are included in this chapter and can be used to create rough drafts to be submitted to the typist who will publish the final document. The worksheets can also be set up as templates committee members use on computers throughout the process.

Issues related to presentation and format need to be addressed as well. The easier it is for the user to read the material on each page, find needed information, and understand the relationships among the parts of each section, the more likely it is that the document will be used by schools and teachers planning classroom experiences. Essential considerations related to presentation and format include the following:

- Pages should be numbered consecutively throughout the document.
- Material presented in chart form is easier for some to grasp than material presented in narrative form.
- Adequate "white space" should be left on each page to facilitate reading.
- Narrative text should be double-spaced.
- Charts and lists should be single-spaced.
- Headings should be used to help the user glance through and understand immediately how the document is structured.
- The print should be of a size that is easy to read.
- Printing on only one side of the page leaves room for teachers to add notes, recommended revisions, and the like.
- Printing different sections on different colors of paper can make each section easier to find.
- Tabs labeled with the name of each section make each section easier to find.
- Using a notebook for binding helps reinforce the idea that the document is a living one to which resource materials can be added.

We once worked with a committee creating language arts curriculum guidelines. A particular concern of that committee was that the guidelines not just be "left on the shelf" or "shoved in a drawer and forgotten." After much careful thought, the committee opted to make the document oversized—11 × 17. A heavy stock cover was used, and metal rings held the document together so that the pages could be laid flat and new pages could be added as necessary. During the year when this document was piloted in the district, this proved to be an example of a good idea that didn't work out as expected. The document was so big that it didn't fit easily in any drawer or on any shelf, nor did it fit easily in anyone's briefcase or book bag. It was unwieldy to hold on one's lap at staff meetings where it was being discussed. The final document was produced in a blue notebook in a standard 8½ × 11-inch size.

THE TITLE PAGE

The title page clearly indicates the curriculum area presented in the guide, the name of the school or district, and the date the document was completed or adopted. Worksheet 6.1 can be used to create the draft of the title page to be submitted to the typist.

THE PREFACE

The preface explains the purpose of the document and how it should be used; describes the process through which it was created; and expresses appreciation to individuals, groups, and organizations that have provided support of any kind throughout the development process. The preface should be short, ideally no longer than one page. Often it is signed by the committee chairperson. Worksheet 6.2 can be used to create the draft of the preface to submit to the typist. Make additional copies of this sheet if more space is needed.

WORKSHEET 6.1 **The Title Page**

Directions to the typist:

- Type only the material that is not included in brackets.
- Center the material on one page.

[School District] _____

_____

[Title] _____

_____

[Date] _____

WORKSHEET 6.2 The Preface

Directions to the typist:

- Type only the material that is not included in brackets.
- Single-space the material.
- Type each section as a separate paragraph.

[What areas of the curriculum and what grade levels are addressed in this document?] The areas of the curriculum and grade levels addressed are _____

_____

_____

_____

[What is the purpose of the document?]

The purpose of this document is to _____

_____

_____

_____

_____

[How is the document meant to be used and by whom?]

This document is meant to be used by _____

_____

_____

_____

_____

[What process was used in developing the document?]

This document was developed through a process involving _____

_____

_____

_____

_____

[To whom should appreciation be expressed?]

The curriculum development committee wishes to express its appreciation to _____

_____

_____

_____

THE LIST OF COMMITTEE MEMBERS

Committee members who participated directly in production of the document should be listed in alphabetical order on a separate page. Special roles played, such as chair of the committee or a subcommittee, should be indicated. The issue of committee members who have dropped out or of others who joined later in the process can sometimes be politically sensitive. You may wish to include dates of service next to the names of committee members.

Worksheet 6.3 can be used to create the list of committee members to be submitted to the typist. Duplicate this sheet if more space is needed.

THE TABLE OF CONTENTS

The table of contents provides an outline of the content of the document and allows the user easy access to any given section. The table of contents should include the title and page number of each section and any subsections. Include each chart as a separate subsection. Worksheet 6.4 can be used to create the draft of the table of contents. Make additional copies of this sheet if more space is needed.

THE GLOSSARY

The glossary defines specialized terms used throughout the document. Providing a glossary prevents confusion and helps to ensure that terms used in the document will be understood by all who use it.

It is helpful throughout the development of the curriculum guidelines to keep a list of terms that should be included in the glossary. It can also be very useful at the end of the process to have someone who has not been involved (a teacher or a community member) read the guidelines and highlight any terms that should be included in the glossary. Worksheet 6.5 can be used to keep a running list of these terms and to create the draft of the glossary to be submitted to the typist. Make additional copies of this sheet if more space is needed.

LISTS OF RESOURCES

Three separate resources lists can be included at the end of the document: a bibliography of materials actually used by the committee, a list of experts consulted, and a list of resources recommended for use by those implementing the curriculum.

The *bibliography* is the listing of all resources actually used during the curriculum development process. Books, articles, papers, and sample curriculum guides from other districts should be included. Any standard bibliography format can be used to list the author(s), title, place of publication, publisher, and date of publication for each printed resource used. If the district has adopted a particular format for students to use, that is the one that should be used for the curriculum guidelines.

The *list of experts consulted* should be presented in alphabetical order by the consultants' last name and should include the name of the consultant, title, organization, area of expertise, nature of the services provided, and the date(s) of those services.

The *list of recommended resources* is an annotated list of resources (print and human) that the curriculum committee believes will be of greatest use to those who are implementing the curriculum. General resources are listed first, with resources for each section of the curriculum document following.

By the time the curriculum development process is completed, it is easy to forget which resources were used or which the committee intended to recommend. It is helpful to keep a running list of those

WORKSHEET 6.3 **The Committee Member List**

Directions to the typist:

- Type only the material that is not included in brackets.
- Single-space the list.
- Type in alphabetical order by last name.

[Name]   [Name]

[Role]   [Role]

[School]   [School]

[Town]   [Town]

[Position]   [Position]

[Name]   [Name]

[Role]   [Role]

[School]   [School]

[Town]   [Town]

[Position]   [Position]

[Name]   [Name]

[Role]   [Role]

[School]   [School]

[Town]   [Town]

[Position]   [Position]

WORKSHEET 6.4   The Table of Contents

Directions to the typist:

- Type only the material that is not included in brackets.
- Single-space each section and double-space between sections.
- Use outline style.

[Page #]

Preface
Committee Members
Table of Contents
   [Section 1]
      [Subsection/Chart A]
      [Subsection/Chart B]
      [Subsection/Chart C]
      [Subsection/Chart D]
      [Subsection/Chart E]
   [Section 2]
      [Subsection/Chart A]
      [Subsection/Chart B]
      [Subsection/Chart C]
      [Subsection/Chart D]
      [Subsection/Chart E]
   [Section 3]
      [Subsection/Chart A]
      [Subsection/Chart B]
      [Subsection/Chart C]
      [Subsection/Chart D]
      [Subsection/Chart E]
   [Section 4]
      [Subsection/Chart A]
      [Subsection/Chart B]
      [Subsection/Chart C]
      [Subsection/Chart D]
      [Subsection/Chart E]
   [Section 5]
      [Subsection/Chart A]
      [Subsection/Chart B]
      [Subsection/Chart C]
      [Subsection/Chart D]
      [Subsection/Chart E]
   [Section 6]
      [Subsection/Chart A]
      [Subsection/Chart B]
      [Subsection/Chart C]
      [Subsection/Chart D]
      [Subsection/Chart E]
   [Section 7]
      [Subsection/Chart A]
      [Subsection/Chart B]
      [Subsection/Chart C]
      [Subsection/Chart D]
      [Subsection/Chart E]
   [Section 8]
      [Subsection/Chart A]
      [Subsection/Chart B]
      [Subsection/Chart C]
      [Subsection/Chart D]
      [Subsection/Chart E]

WORKSHEET 6.5 The Glossary

Directions to the typist:

- Type only the material that is not included in brackets.
- Place terms in alphabetical order.
- Single-space each section and double-space between sections.
- Boldface or underline the term to be defined.

Glossary

[Term] _____

[Definition] _____

_____

_____

[Term] _____

[Definition] _____

_____

_____

[Term] _____

[Definition] _____

_____

_____

used by the full committee or subcommittees. Worksheets 6.6, 6.7, and 6.8 can be used for this purpose, as well as to create the final drafts to be submitted to the typist. Make additional copies of these sheets if more space is needed.

APPENDICES

Appendices can be included at the time of publication of the document or later. These may include many different kinds of materials—assessment tools, lists of best practices, suggested materials, and so forth. It is important, though, that you consider carefully what will actually be included. Bulky appendices can make the document quite lengthy and therefore threatening to the new user.

POSTING ON THE DISTRICT'S WEB SITE

Although most teachers like to have a hard copy of the parts of the curriculum guidelines for which they are responsible, it is important also to publish these documents and associated resources on the schools' and district's Web sites. The format many teachers favor is a chart or table on which they can see a link to the scope and sequence for each subject area they are responsible to teach. An example that works well comes from the Enlarged City School District of Middletown, as shown in Figure 6.1.

All sections of the curriculum guidelines should be available electronically. A choice needs to be made about whether to post the documents as word processing documents, as PDF (portable document format) files, or simply as electronic links. Each choice has advantages and disadvantages, as shown in Figure 6.2.

Some districts provide all three—electronic links, word processing documents, and PDF files—to accommodate varying preferences and styles of teachers.

CELEBRATING RESULTS

Once the curriculum guidelines have been developed and published, the curriculum development committee needs to celebrate the end of its task. Such celebration serves three major purposes:

1. It brings closure to the process of development, belying the perception that "around here nothing ever gets done."

2. It recognizes the importance and value of participation in the development process.

3. It reinforces the worth of the curriculum product itself.

Celebration need not be grandiose or formal, but it does require planning. While there are countless ways to celebrate results of curriculum development, we have found the following to be particularly beneficial:

1. Pay attention to the end product. A standard we use is that any writer of the curriculum should be able to display the curriculum on his or her coffee table. We've never met anyone who wished to do so, but the standard helps to maintain quality control.

2. Provide extra copies of the curriculum to participants at a free or reduced rate. Participants may wish to share copies with colleagues in other schools, place a copy in their professional development portfolios, or share it in graduate courses, for example. Offering several free copies to the authors is a standard publishing practice and a good model for curriculum developers.

(Text continues on page 109)

WORKSHEET 6.6 The Bibliography

Directions to the typist:

- Type only the material that is not included in brackets.
- Use a standard bibliography format to present the material.
- Single-space the bibliography.

[Author(s)] _____

[Title] _____

[Publisher] _____

[Place of publication] _____

[Date of publication] _____

[Volume] _____ [Page numbers] _____

[Other] _____

[Author(s)] _____

[Title] _____

[Publisher] _____

[Place of publication] _____

[Date of publication] _____

[Volume] _____ [Page numbers] _____

[Other] _____

WORKSHEET 6.7 The List of Experts Consulted

Directions to the typist:

- Type only the material that is not included in brackets.
- Present material in alphabetical order by consultants' last name.
- Single-space each entry and double-space between entries.

[Name of consultant] _____

[Title] _____

[Organization/affiliation] _____

[Nature of services provided] _____

[Date(s)] _____

[Name of consultant] _____

[Title] _____

[Organization/affiliation] _____

[Nature of services provided] _____

[Date(s)] _____

WORKSHEET 6.8 Recommended Resources

Directions to the typist:

- Type only the material that is not included in brackets.
- Use a standard bibliography format to present the material.
- Group entries by heading indicated, but type each heading only once.
- Single-space each entry and double-space between entries.

[Heading] _____

[Author(s)] _____

[Title] _____

[Publisher] _____

[Place of publication] _____

[Date of publication] _____

[Volume] _____ [Page numbers] _____

[URL] _____

[Other] _____

[Annotation] _____

Figure 6.1 Enlarged City School District of Middletown Sample Scope and Sequence Links

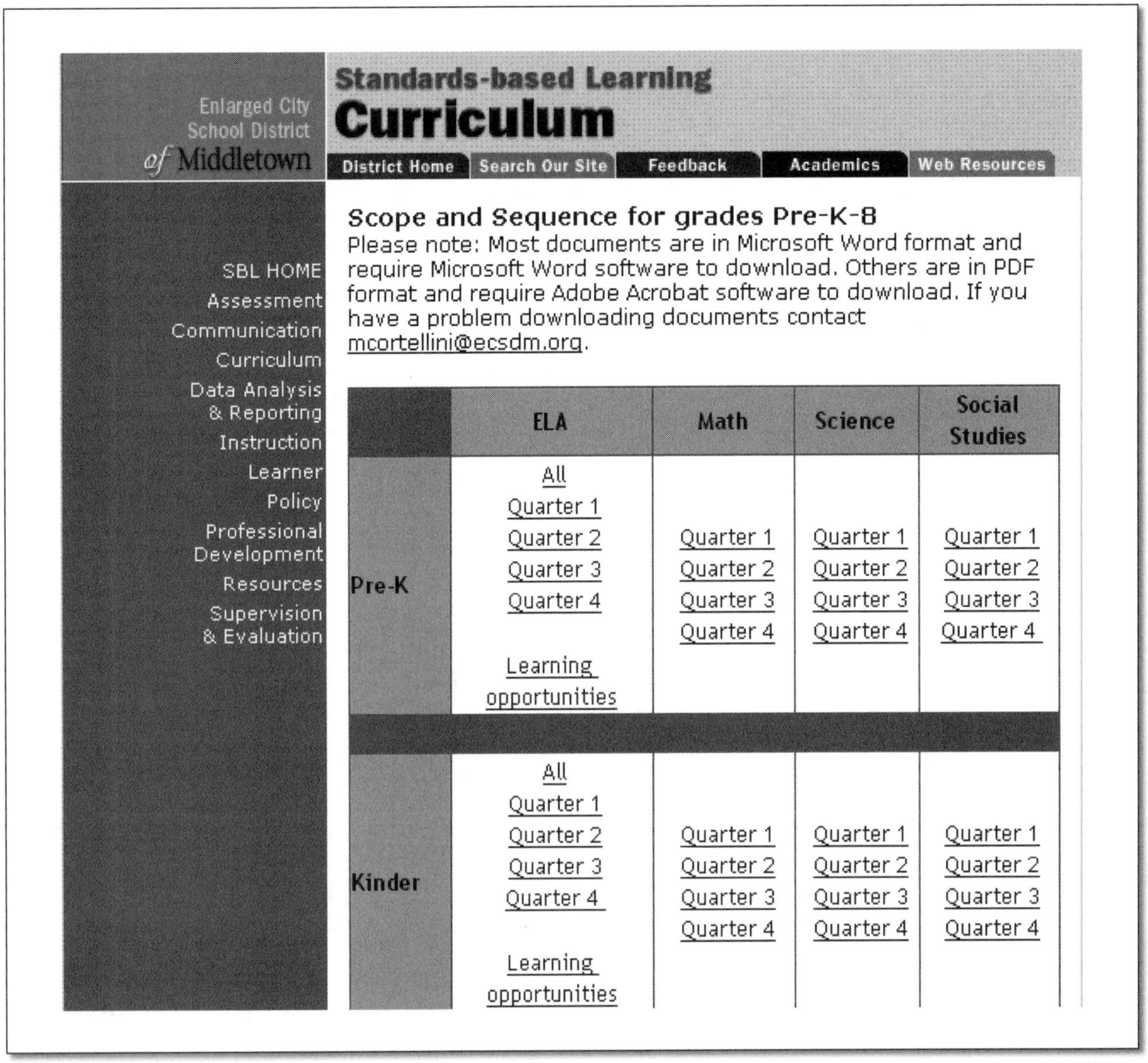
Enlarged City School District of Middletown

Standards-based Learning

Curriculum

District Home | Search Our Site | Feedback | Academics | Web Resources

SBL HOME
Assessment
Communication
Curriculum
Data Analysis & Reporting
Instruction
Learner
Policy
Professional Development
Resources
Supervision & Evaluation

Scope and Sequence for grades Pre-K-8

Please note: Most documents are in Microsoft Word format and require Microsoft Word software to download. Others are in PDF format and require Adobe Acrobat software to download. If you have a problem downloading documents contact mcortellini@ecsdm.org.

	ELA	Math	Science	Social Studies
Pre-K	All Quarter 1 Quarter 2 Quarter 3 Quarter 4 Learning opportunities	Quarter 1 Quarter 2 Quarter 3 Quarter 4	Quarter 1 Quarter 2 Quarter 3 Quarter 4	Quarter 1 Quarter 2 Quarter 3 Quarter 4
Kinder	All Quarter 1 Quarter 2 Quarter 3 Quarter 4 Learning opportunities	Quarter 1 Quarter 2 Quarter 3 Quarter 4	Quarter 1 Quarter 2 Quarter 3 Quarter 4	Quarter 1 Quarter 2 Quarter 3 Quarter 4

Used with permission of the Enlarged City School District of Middletown, NY.

3. Share copies with the profession. Quality curriculum work deserves dissemination. Make certain that the professional library in each school has a copy of each set of curriculum guidelines and maintain a curriculum library in public view in the central office.

4. Provide copies for curriculum libraries at your state department of education and at colleges and universities in your area.

5. Display your curriculum at the annual conference of the Association for Supervision and Curriculum Development (ASCD) (application forms for this purpose are available from ASCD) and at meetings of other relevant professional organizations, such as the National

Figure 6.2 Advantages and Disadvantages to Three Formats for Posting Electronically

Formats	Advantages	Disadvantages
Word processing document	• Easy for users to add materials, examples, links in their planning • Prints in a user-friendly format	• Key elements (e.g., performance indicators) can be moved or changed • Some users may not have the necessary word processing program
Acrobat PDF file	• Key material cannot easily be changed • Program needed to open the file is available for free • File prints in a user-friendly format • Can link table of contents to move around easily	• Tables and such cannot expand to accommodate users who wish to do their planning electronically
Electronic link	• No software compatibility issues • Resources and materials can be directly linked to standards and performance indicators	• Often will not print out in a user-friendly format

Council of Teachers of Mathematics and the National Council of Teachers of English. You may also wish to feature your curriculum in conference presentations, regional or statewide inservice events, and other professional gatherings. The point is, make sure your work is shared and valued.

6. Recognize curriculum development committee members through letters or certificates. Make certain that the principal, superintendent, school board members, professional association, and others recognize the work of each committee member. If the district has a formal recognition process, consider committee members for recognition.

7. Provide members with a memento of participation. Examples we've seen include a coffee mug, a book, a membership in a professional organization, a voucher for a conference, and a gift certificate.

8. Make your final meeting together a celebration. This can take the form of coffee and cake at the end of the last regular meeting, refreshments at a local establishment, or a group dinner including spouses. In any case, make sure that your final meeting ends on a festive note.

Use Worksheet 6.9 to plan ways to celebrate completion of the development of your K–12 curriculum guidelines.

The celebration brings closure to this phase of the process as you turn your attention to making the guidelines a reality in every classroom in the school or district through the process of implementation.

WORKSHEET 6.9 Celebrating Results

Instructions: Use this worksheet to plan ways to celebrate completion of the K–12 curriculum guidelines. The chairperson may wish to complete this worksheet alone; however, input should be elicited from curriculum development committee members.

1. The document(s) will be posted at the following places on district and school Web sites:

   _____

2. Each committee member will receive _____ copies of the K–12 curriculum guidelines free of charge and may receive additional copies for $_____ each.

3. The document will be disseminated to the following:

   • Professional Libraries (list)

   • Professional Organizations (list)

   • Individuals (list)

4. The following individuals will be asked to formally recognize the work of the committee:

   ____ Superintendent

   ____ Principal for each member

   ____ School board chair and members

   ____ Other (list)

5. Each member will receive the following memento for participation: _____

6. Our final meeting celebration will be: _____

7

Development of Common Assessments

A Design Overview

Once the curriculum guidelines are completed, published, and celebrated, common assessments can be created to align with the scope and sequence in the curriculum guidelines. Common assessments are typically developed by grade-level teams, middle-level content teams, and high school departments. These assessments are common in these ways:

- They are grounded in common standards and performance indicators.
- They are administered by all teachers in the grade level or content area.
- They have common items.
- They are scored using common scoring protocols.

These assessments can impact curriculum implementation and instructional leadership in these ways:

- Aligning curriculum with standards
- Reaching consensus on priorities for instruction and assessment
- Pacing curriculum implementation
- Generating discussion and building common language among educators and students

Common local assessments can also be powerful tools for preparing for statewide assessments and can provide a common context for reporting student performance.

Typically, common local assessments are utilized for three purposes:

- *Common diagnostic assessments* help to determine prior student learning and to make initial decisions related to level of instruction, grouping, and instructional strategies. These assessments are typically administered at the outset of the school year or unit of study and when new students enroll.

- *Common formative assessments* provide information to students and educators during the teaching/learning process and provide important information for differentiating instruction. These assessments are typically embedded in instruction and may take the form of "testlets"—brief, focused assessments providing immediate feedback on narrowly defined standards or curriculum.

- *Common summative assessments* provide information as to how well students have done and provide information for student-level decision making, for grading and reporting student progress, and for program evaluation. These are typically designed to be administered at the end of a unit, end of quarter or semester, or end of the course.

Designing common local assessments typically requires a greater level of technical rigor than individual teacher-developed assessments but a lesser level of rigor than statewide assessments used to provide rewards or sanctions to students or schools, assessments utilized to identify students with disabilities or students considered gifted or talented, or to answer other eligibility questions. In general, the level of technical rigor required becomes greater as the consequences for the student increase.

This chapter provides an overview of a process we use to design common local assessments. This is by no means the only procedure possible or necessarily the best procedure in every situation. The purposes of the chapter are to highlight considerations when developing common assessments and to provide a base procedure that can be modified and improved locally.

The order in which the process is presented is logical rather than chronological. In practice, the process is iterative and will not always follow the order represented. While the process is presented in briefly described steps, each step requires considerable thought, research, and attention to detail and quality control.

ASSESSMENT DESIGN

Step 1: Define Purpose

Clearly define the purposes of the common assessment. Is it diagnostic, formative, or summative?

Common *diagnostic* assessments provide common information as to the current status of student learning in relation to standards. These assessments are typically administered at the beginning and end of the school year or semester and when new students enter the school and form the basis for placement and referrals to support programs.

Common *formative assessments* provide ongoing information related to key standards being emphasized in instruction and form the basis for dialogue regarding instructional improvement.

Common *summative assessments* provide information on students' achievement status or growth over time. They also may help to prepare students for high stakes assessment such as state assessments and the Advanced Placement Program. How will the results be used by students? By teachers? By the school or district? By others? Figure 7.1 lists ways that common assessment results may be used by each of these subgroups.

Step 2: Identify "Fair Game" in Terms of Standards

Which standards are "fair game," meaning that they *may* be assessed? Note that all standards that are fair game are not necessarily assessed. One reason for this has to do with the length of the assessment, the potential of testing fatigue among students, and the amount of time devoted to assessment in the school year. Another reason relates to the demands on teachers, data experts, and others in the system. These demands include time to score assessments, to input and analyze results, and to translate the data into priorities.

Figure 7.1 Use of Common Assessments

User Group	Uses
Students	• Receive feedback on learning related to standards • Clarify expectations as to what content is deemed most important • Practice skills and assessment strategies that may transfer to other assessments
Teachers	• Receive information related to performance of their students that can drive instruction • Develop shared understanding of relative importance of standards to be measured • Gain knowledge and technical expertise in assessment design, administration, and scoring • Can predict how well students will do on other assessments • Can provide information for grading and reporting
Administrators	• Provide context for professional dialogue related to standards and performance • Receive information related to performance of groups and subgroups prior to high stakes assessment • Receive information for data-driven decision making

A third reason is that some standards predict success on other standards well enough that the latter do not need to be directly assessed. For example, at the fifth- or sixth-grade level, subtraction of whole numbers may not be directly assessed since it can be assessed through division. Worksheet 7.1 provides a tool to record the purpose of your assessment and the standards and performance indicators from your scope and sequence that are fair game.

Step 3: Balance of Representation

What is the relative weight to be assigned to each standard or (more commonly) standards cluster? For example, a social studies assessment might be 40% history, 30% geography, 20% economics, and 10% civics. The balance of representation should reflect the relative importance of the standards or standard cluster *for this assessment*, based on the emphasis of the unit, the marking period, or the course. This will vary, for example, from unit to unit, marking period to marking period, and course to course. Often, however, the balance of representation is set to mirror that of the statewide assessment.

The balance of representation becomes part of the assessment blueprint, as discussed in Step 4 below. An example is embedded in the blueprint shown in Figure 7.2. Use Worksheet 7.2 to develop and record the balance of representation.

Step 4: Develop an Assessment Blueprint

What item types will be included in the assessment and in what proportion? Common item types include the following:

- *Multiple choice items* can be used to cover a wide range of content. They are efficient in that they take relatively little time to answer (usually one minute or less) or to score.
- *Short-answer items* are best used to assess defined problems with limited solutions, such as math computation. They typically take 2 to 5 minutes to answer. Students must demonstrate knowledge and skills by generating rather than selecting an answer.

WORKSHEET 7.1 **Purpose and Fair Game**

Purposes of the common assessment (check all that apply)	____ Diagnostic ____ Formative ____ Summative	____ Placement ____ Instructional decision making ____ Grading/reporting ____ Program evaluation ____ Other
Projected users of results	____ Students ____ Teachers ____ Parents ____ Administrators ____ Evaluators ____ Other	
Standards that are fair game for this assessment	Number or label	Descriptor
[Add rows as needed]		

Figure 7.2 Statement of Purpose and Assessment Blueprint

Purpose

The purpose of the assessment will be summative, with information from it to be used both for student-level decision making and for program evaluation. The group discussed whether the results would be used to help make decisions about placement in Grade 7 math classes. No decision was made on this question yet, but the group agreed to revisit this question later.

The audience for the assessment results will be teachers, students, administrators, parents, and the wider public.

Fair Game

The power standards will be the fair game for the assessments. The group *may* decide to use a subset of these. (Note: Prior to developing the common assessments, the district identified *power standards* [Reeves, 2005] for each grade level.)

Grade Levels

The group agreed to begin developing assessments for Grades 3 and 6 simultaneously.

Time of Assessment Administration

The group agreed that these assessments will be administered in the spring.

The group discussed the balance of representation for the assessments and decided on the following:

	Grade 3		Grade 6	
	NECAP (% of points)	*ANESU* (% of points)	*NECAP* (% of points)	*ANESU* (% of points)
Umbrella (cut across all content areas [e.g., labeling data])		20		20
Number and operations	60	50	35	30
Geometry and measurement	15	10	25	20
Probability and statistics	10	10	10	10
Functions and algebra	15	10	30	20

The group made further decisions about the *blueprint* for the assessments as follows:

    Grade 3—60 minutes (more time if student is working productively) administered in two 30-minute sections.
        First sitting (day 1):
            Multiple choice—15 minutes (15 items) (develop or find 30 items)
            Extended response—15 minutes (1 item) (develop or find 3 items)
        Second sitting (day 2):
            Short answer—30 minutes (20 items) (develop or find 40 items)

    Grade 6—

    90 minutes (more time if student is working productively) administered in two 45-minute sections
        First sitting (day 1)
            Multiple choice—10 minutes (10 items)
               (develop or find 20 items)
            Short answer—20 minutes (15 items)
               (develop or find 50 items total for day 1 and day 2)
            Extended response—15 minutes (1 item: numbers and operations)
               (develop or find 2 items)
        Second sitting
            Multiple choice—10 minutes (10 items)
               (develop or find 20 items)
             Short answer—20 minutes (15 items)
               (develop or find 50 items total for day 1 and day 2)
            Extended response—15 minutes (1 item: functions and algebra)
               (develop or find 2 items)

Source: Addison Northeast Supervisory Union, 2006. Used with permission.

WORKSHEET 7.2 Balance of Representation

1. What are the standard clusters that you will use to organize the balance of representation?

Example (science)	Biology, chemistry, physics, earth science, inquiry
Example (English language arts)	Reading, listening, writing, speaking
Example (social studies)	History, geography, economics, government
Example (mathematics)	Numbers and operation, functions and algebra, geometry and measurement, probability and statistics

2. What percentage of the assessment will be allocated to each standard cluster (must total 100%)?

Cluster	Percentage

- *Constructed response items* typically require students to apply higher-order thinking skills, such as analysis, synthesis, and evaluation. They take 5 to 10 minutes to complete. These items are often scored using a rubric, and scoring training and calibration are essential.
- *Extended response items* also assess higher-order thinking, often involve multiple solutions, and require the student to justify the answer. These items take typically 10 to 20 minutes to complete and also require careful scorer training and calibration.

Decisions regarding item types for local common assessments require considering the standards assessed, the assessment time available, and the investment of time and effort in scoring. For example, given a 90-minute assessment block, a high school science assessment might include 20 multiple choice items, 5 short answers, 3 constructed responses, and 1 extended response.

An additional decision is whether the assessment is timed (in this example, everyone finished at the end of 90 minutes) or open-ended (90 minutes is expected but students can work as long as they are working productively).

The assessment blueprint will connect the standards being assessed to the items and item types to be selected or developed. Figure 7.2 is an example of an assessment blueprint for a Grade 6 end-of-year common mathematics assessment.

Worksheet 7.3 provides a planning tool that you may use in developing a blueprint for your common assessment.

Step 5: Select or Develop Items

If high quality items exist and are available, it is almost always best to use them rather than create new items. This is why access to release items or item banks is of immeasurable value. Many states and test publishers release items on the statewide assessments each year. Some states, like New York, release all items each year. In other cases, like the New England Common Assessment, a subset of items (in New England, one third) is released each year. Release items can usually be found at the state's or publisher's Web site.

Many publishers have developed sets of items known as item banks. These are commercially available, usually by subscription, although some item banks are in the public domain. Item banks are typically organized so that they can be sorted by multiple variables such as grade level, content area, and standards or performance indicators.

However, it is often necessary to create items to meet your individual needs. In initially selecting or developing items, it is best to select many more items than you will actually need—you may want three times as many depending on the importance of the assessment. Make sure that you have enough items so that there is a reasonable expectation that you can fill your assessment blueprint. If, for example, the blueprint calls for 20 multiple choice items, you may need 50 to 60. If you will need two extended response items, you may start with six.

Step 6: Field Testing Items

Field testing allows you to see how the item actually behaves with your students and provides item statistics that can let you make decisions as to which items to include in the assessment. Again, field testing is most practical, and most important, with high stakes summative assessment. You should field test all your items. Because you have more items than you will use, you may give subsets of items to different students. There are several statistics that can be used to judge the appropriateness of items. Here are a few:

Item Difficulty

For multiple choice or short answer items, divide the number of correct responses by total responses. The range is from 0.00 to 1.00. A rule of thumb is that items with less than .20 are too hard and items with greater than .90 are too easy.

WORKSHEET 7.3 Assessment Blueprint

Item Type	Number of Items	Number of Points
Multiple choice		
Short answer		
Constructed response		
Extended response		

Timing and Logistics	Notes
Number of sittings	
Duration of sittings	
Items per sitting (by item type)	
Points per sitting (by item type)	
Items per sitting (by item type)	
Location of assessment	
Materials provided by teachers	
Other materials allowed/disallowed	
Modifications permitted	
Accommodations permitted	

For constructed responses scored with a rubric, calculate the average score on the item. For example, if you use a rubric from 0 (no response) to 4 (exceeding standard), items less than .80 may be too hard and items greater than 3.60 may be too easy.

Item Discrimination (r)

For both multiple choice and constructed response items, calculate the correlation (r) between the item and the total score. Students scoring higher on the entire assessment should score higher on the item. The range is –1.00 to 1.00. For multiple choice, the correlation should be .20 or higher. For constructed response, it should be .30 or higher.

For example, suppose that on a social studies common assessment there is a data-based quest that is an extended response item and is scored using a four-point rubric. If students receiving 3s and 4s on this item also perform well on the entire exam (as is often the case), there would be a positive correlation.

Bias

You can determine item bias between groups—for example, males and females. To do this, you compare performance of males and females who performed on the entire assessment with performance on the item. There shouldn't be more than 10% difference. If, for example, an item relates to an aspect of popular culture, it may favor one ethnicity—perhaps Caucasian learners. If African-American, Caucasian, and Hispanic students scored equally well on the entire assessment but Caucasians scored 20 points higher on an item, the item may be biased.

Step 7: Develop the Assessment

When you have enough strong items to fill your blueprint, you are ready to construct the assessment. If not, you will need to select or develop more items.

Be careful not to select all very difficult or all very easy items. Use the item difficulty and item discrimination data that you gathered in your field test to build a balanced assessment, having already eliminated those items that do not work.

Another check on item balance is *cognitive complexity*, also referred to as *depth of knowledge*. Webb (2002) has proposed four levels of depth of knowledge:

- Level 1: Recall (e.g., fact, definition, procedure). Requires student to demonstrate a rote response, perform an algorithm, follow a set procedure, or perform a defined series of steps.
- Level 2: Decision making beyond rote response. May require, for example, classifying information, interpreting, explaining, and describing.
- Level 3: Requires reasoning, planning, and use of evidence. Students might draw conclusions, cite evidence, or develop a logical argument.
- Level 4: Generally involves work over an extended period of time and is often assessed through exhibitions and portfolios. Generally requires making connections and synthesizing ideas. Most often Level 4 assessment is individualized and not part of a common assessment (though there may be a common expectation and even a common rubric).

Contrary to a common belief, item type does not determine depth of knowledge. It is possible to develop multiple choice, short answer, and constructed response items at Levels 1, 2, and 3. The following are examples of constructed response science items developed at the three levels.

Level 1: Write a sentence defining Newton's Second Law of Motion.

Level 2: Explain an example of momentum.

Level 3: Given a GrowLab and set of bean seeds, develop research questions and a scientific investigation to determine the impact of light on growth of the bean plants.

Use Worksheet 7.4 to describe the depth of knowledge of the items in your assessment.

WORKSHEET 7.4 Depth of Knowledge

Item Type	Level 1 Items	Level 2 Items	Level 3 Items	Level 4 Items
Multiple Choice				
Short Answer				
Constructed Response				
Extended Response				

Step 8: Administer and Score the Assessment

For common assessments to be truly common, you need to set up common protocols for administration. These may include, for example, a common set of instructions, common protocols for response to students' questions, materials allowable (such as dictionaries, calculators, or computers), For example, students may be permitted access to any materials that are in their classrooms on a daily basis. Or teachers may agree that student questions related to pronunciation of words may be permitted during math assessment but not reading assessment.

If the assessment includes constructed or extended response items, it is important to train and calibrate scorers (see also Step 4). This process typically involves these steps:

- Review of scoring guides (if they exist) or drafting of scoring guides; agreement on criteria and common terms
- Selection of anchor papers that are clearly exemplars of each level
- Individual scoring using anchor papers
- Group discussion of similarities and differences in scores (this step is excellent professional development and can lead to high levels of consensus and inter-rater reliability)
- Individual scoring often supplemental by double scoring a sample (perhaps 10%); scoring is often accomplished in table groups with a table leader doing double scoring or "read-behind" scoring

Step 9: Set Cut Scores

If the assessment is tied to grades, you will need to make decisions as to what performance level is needed for each grade. Common assessments are often tied to grades for older students to provide incentive to perform well. At all levels, these assessments may provide strong, standards-based information that can support accurate grading. The common assessments may also provide information that reduces the need for additional assessment and unnecessary repetition. Conversely, assessments that are formative in nature and therefore primarily intended to drive instruction are often not included in grading because the performance occurs partway into the learning process.

If the common assessment is to be included in grading, this is typically done by setting *cut scores*. These scores represent the upper and lower limits of performance leading to a given grade. For example a score of between 30 and 49 might translate to a grade of B. Sometimes cut scores are established for subtests. For example, to receive an A, a student may need to earn a certain number of total points *and* perform at Level 3 or higher on a writing prompt. For assessments to be common, these must be the same across teachers and sections of students.

CONCLUSION

The purpose of this chapter is to provide a brief introduction to developing common assessments. As stated at the outset, these steps are not intended for classroom assessment or even for all common assessments. The degree of rigor required increases based on the importance of the consequences for the students.

This chapter refers to procedures, such as calibration, item analysis, and setting cut scores, that are complex and require much more thought and consideration. As well, there are aspects of assessment design, such as universal design and developing alternative assessments that are not discussed at all.

The purpose here is to frame planning of common assessments with due consideration for the complexities of the process and to provide information for assessment decision making. Ultimately, considering these issues can lead both to strong common assessments and to increased assessment knowledge and skills to impact classroom and statewide assessment.

8

Planning for Implementation

This chapter will lead you through a process of planning for implementation of the curriculum guidelines that has proven highly successful in our work with schools and districts. The steps of the planning process are outlined in Figure 8.1.

Figure 8.1 Planning for Implementation

Step 1. Identifying leadership teams

Step 2. Defining roles and responsibilities in the planning process

Step 3. Determining priorities and focus areas

Step 4. Developing SMART goals

Step 5. Developing implementation goals

Step 6. Developing the implementation plan—components, timelines, roles, and responsibilities

Step 7. Communicating the plan

Source: Center for Curriculum Renewal, 2008

Although presenting as linear, the implementation process is in fact recursive. The steps described herein will spiral as implementation progresses and new challenges and successes inform the process.

STEP 1: IDENTIFYING LEADERSHIP TEAMS

Support of implementation may require participation of multiple existing and new leadership teams, especially in districts committed to collaboration and building professional learning communities. For example, implementation of new curriculum guidelines may fall within the purview of each of these existing structures and possibly more:

- Building-based grade-level teams
- Middle school interdisciplinary teams
- High school departments
- Building- and district-based administrative teams
- District professional development committee
- District mentoring and new teacher support teams
- Building design teams

Furthermore, there may be a need to create a new structure to support implementation of a specific curriculum. An example of creating a new leadership structure in the South Burlington (Vermont) School District is presented in Figure 8.2.

You will note that, in this case, the district created two distinct teams with some overlapping membership. The steering committee is balanced among administrators, teachers, and teacher leaders and provides strong administrative and organizational support to move implementation forward. The math committee is composed of teacher leaders, facilitators, and classroom teachers and supports the actual implementation of the curriculum in each classroom.

Worksheet 8.1 provides a tool for you to identify the key leadership teams in your school or district that will be responsible for leading implementation.

STEP 2: DEFINING ROLES AND RESPONSIBILITIES IN THE PLANNING PROCESS

Our experience is that the building design team—a team consisting of the building administrators, key teacher leaders, support services staff, parents, and frequently students and whose role is to provide overall focus and direction in relation to improving student performance—should take the overall lead for implementation at the school level. As such, they are the ideal team to lead implementation planning.

If there are no building design teams in your district, you may need to look to alternative existing groups, such as the principal's cabinet, the content area leaders, or the department chairpersons to lead this process of defining roles and responsibilities. Or a design team may be formed. In any case, building leadership must be directly involved in the process. Teachers and support staff involved should be recognized faculty leaders. Members should be strong collaborators and should be actively using student performance data to drive instruction.

It is the job of the building design team, or its counterpart, to define roles and responsibilities for implementation at the building level. For example, departments may take responsibility for selection of materials and resources: the district professional development committee may plan districtwide professional development; and the administrative team may take the lead on incorporating implementation issues in walk-throughs, goal setting, and other supervision processes.

The district leadership team is responsible for establishing parameters within which building-based decisions may occur. This team is also responsible for monitoring overall progress over time and to provide support and resources to the building planning or design teams. District personnel

Figure 8.2 Example: Creating a New Leadership Structure

South Burlington School District

Mathematics Implementation Plan

2007–2008

Roles and Responsibilities

To provide support, direction, and oversight of the mathematics program implementation, local comprehensive assessment plan, and professional development, we have created two committees. Please review the purpose of each item below.

Steering Committee

The steering committee is composed of all elementary principals, teacher leaders, assistant superintendent for instruction, and building-based teacher representatives. A consultant joins the committee on request. The purpose of the steering committee is to provide oversight, direction, and support of the mathematics committee and also to monitor program implementation and determine next steps.

Mathematics Committee

The mathematics committee is composed mainly of classroom teachers and math teacher leaders. The committee is chaired by the two teacher leaders. A consultant will provide training and support to this committee for the 2007–2008 school year. The purpose of the mathematics committee is to develop our local assessment plan and to make recommendations about the schedule of administration and process for analyzing results to the steering committee.

Mathematics Facilitators

- Attend three facilitator support meetings and professional development sessions (September, January, and March)
- Facilitate building-based grade-level or grade-cluster dialogue about the mathematics program
- Provide input to the math committee and steering committee about professional development and program implementation needs of staff
- At grade-level and building meetings, assist in the collection of data that will inform the implementation process

Math Coaches

- Collect information from schools to assist with materials distribution and program implementation
- Attend publisher trainings
- Work with consultant and math committee to further develop our comprehensive local assessment system
- Co-chair math committee, build agendas, create and distribute minutes
- Participate on the steering committee
- Develop protocols and topics for ongoing dialogue at school level
- Support and train teacher facilitators
- Visit classrooms and support teachers at the time of instruction
- Develop process for ongoing collection of information
- Inform steering committee about professional development needs of teachers
- Develop and use group facilitation skills and use protocols to examine student work
- Inform and support data collection process

Principals

- Ongoing learning about math content and pedagogy
- Monitor program implementation
- Support teacher leaders and facilitators
- Participate on the steering committee
- Schedule and ensure monthly building-based dialogue about program implementation
- Ensure that relevant information is shared with whole faculty resulting from the math committee and steering committee work
- Inform and support the data collection process

Assistant Superintendent for Instruction

- Oversee process of program implementation
- Schedule all professional development
- Order program materials and coordinate the distribution process
- Support teacher leaders, math facilitators, and principals
- Chair the math steering committee
- Set up process to discuss content and program coordination with the middle school level
- Monitor and support the work of the math committee
- Develop a system for collection and use of a wide range of teacher and student data

---

Used with permission of the South Burlington School District, Vermont.

WORKSHEET 8.1 Key Leadership Teams

Identify the key existing leadership teams that will be responsible for leading aspects of implementation. See examples on page 123 of Chapter 8.

Existing Leadership Team(s)	Key Players

Potential New Leadership Team(s)	Key Players

are also responsible for generating relevant student achievement data to drive decision making. Use Worksheet 8.2 to record decisions related to roles and responsibilities in the implementation process.

STEP 3: DETERMINING PRIORITIES AND FOCUS AREAS

A useful construct for determining priorities and focus areas is the no choice/guided choice/free choice continuum. *No choice* priorities may be determined by law, regulation, school board policy, or established district practice. For example, all new teachers may be required to participate in 10 hours of technology training in the first semester of the first year. Parameters may also be set by the superintendent or district level staff based on critical need defined by student performance. They may be set by the principal based on building needs.

Guided choice provides broad categories that each school is expected to address in implementation. Within the category, the school may select specific aspects for focus.

Free choice items may be determined for the whole school by the building design team or may be left to individuals or collaborative groups, such as study groups, to determine for themselves.

Figure 8.3 represents the no choice/guided choice/free choice continuum established for a school district planning implementation for a particular school year.

Use Worksheet 8.3 to record the priorities and focus areas determined for the planning process.

STEP 4: DEVELOPING SMART GOALS

In implementation planning, we find it useful to distinguish between SMART results goals that are explicitly linked to student performance and implementation goals that support the attainment of these results goals.

SMART goals are defined by their acronym as Strategic/Specific, Measurable, Attainable/Aligned, Results focused, and Time bound (Roy, 2007; Summers, 2008).

SMART goals are strategic and specific in that they narrow the focus to a few well-defined areas based on the performance of students. Most schools and districts take on so many goals that, in effect, they have none. SMART goals are intentionally selected for the potential for the greatest impact on the most important areas of student performance.

They are measurable in that they specify the targets for student learning and the tools that will be used to measure that performance. They are attainable in that there is a reasonable expectation that the targets can and will be met. They are time bound in that they identify the time allocated for attaining results.

In working with schools and districts, we find it much more productive to begin with SMART goals rather than implementation goals. First, the SMART goals establish the focus on student performance. Planners begin with results, not with activities. Second, a single implementation strategy may impact multiple student performance results. Planning for professional development, supervision, and colleague support is more efficient when the end is determined first. For example, implementation of a research-based instructional strategy such as *objectives and feedback* (Marzano, 2003) will support increased student performance across grade levels and content areas.

The first step in developing SMART goals is review of student performance data. Central office staff should provide data related to the performance data. Data should be disaggregated in terms of subgroups such as poverty, ethnicity, or disability. When possible, longitudinal data should be provided to track performance over time.

Worksheet 8.4 provides key questions to guide selection of focus areas based on your data.

Once focus areas are determined, SMART goals are frequently developed using a tree diagram. Figure 8.4 provides an example of a tree diagram for a SMART English language arts goal. Note that the goal is built using targets, measures, and indicators. Note also that the goal is specific as to student performance, measurable, aligned with an important and worthy goal (increased performance in English language arts), presumably attainable, results oriented, and time bound. The SMART goal is supported by implementation goals (five are included in this example). We will return to implementation goals in a later section.

WORKSHEET 8.2 Roles and Responsibilities

Identify the roles and responsibilities proposed for key existing and potential leadership teams identified on Worksheet 8.1.

Existing Leadership Team(s)	Potential Roles and Responsibilities in Implementation	Agreement as to Accepting These Roles (record date and person(s) agreeing)

Potential New Leadership Team(s)	Potential Roles and Responsibilities in Implementation	Agreement as to Accepting These Roles (record date and person(s) agreeing)

Figure 8.3 No Choice/Guided Choice/Free Choice

An Example		
(Note: As presented to school—school will make guided choices and free choices)		
School: Ernie Davis Middle School, Elmira, NY		

No Choice—Must Implement	*Guided Choice—Must Implement Selected Aspects (select)*	*Free Choice (add)*
Win/win student management program	Family engagement	
Curriculum webs in English language arts and mathematics	Classroom assessment/ assessment for learning	
Research-based instructional strategies—objectives and feedback, homework and practice, questioning		

Source: Elmira City School District, NY. Used with permission.

Worksheet 8.5 is a blank tree diagram. Please note that the number of boxes for targets, measures, and indicators are arbitrary: you may have a different number. However, the principle of multiple measures applies; indicators of success are much more robust when more than one measure confirms the results.

Make several copies of this tool as you begin to develop tree diagrams and establish SMART goals. While you may want to practice on your own, this is work best done in teams. You should create one copy of Worksheet 8.5 for each SMART goal.

STEP 5: DEVELOPING IMPLEMENTATION GOALS

Implementation goals specify processes, programs, and practices supporting the attainment of the SMART goals. Often these goals define the behaviors and skill sets for adults creating the learning environment for students. In the example in Figure 8.4, both implementation goals relate to teachers. Others may relate to supervisors, mentors, coaches, parents, and others directly or indirectly supporting student learning.

Implementation goals may specify desirable adult behaviors as a result of professional development, supervision, and colleague support. However, implementation goals do not specify these activities themselves. The following is an example of an appropriate implementation goal: "By the end of the year, all supervisors will be providing regular feedback to all teachers about their use of objectives and feedback in their classrooms." This is in contrast to the expression of an activity, such as "By the end of the year, all supervisors will have completed walk-through training." Implementation goals have to do with use of desired practices in classrooms and schools, with the ultimate goal being routine use in all classrooms throughout the school.

Implementation goals link to and support specific SMART goals, as in Figure 8.4. However, implementation goals frequently support more than one SMART goal at the same time. Thus we find it useful to have participants articulate the implementation goals on a sheet separate from the SMART goals. This helps in making connections across goals and increasing efficiency in implementation. Just as the SMART goals should be carefully selected and few in number, so should the implementation goals for processes, programs, and practices.

Worksheet 8.6 is designed to record implementation goals that cut across the SMART goals in your implementation plan.

Once you have identified these, return to the copies of Worksheet 8.5 (you should have one per SMART goal) and determine whether any implementation goals unique to that SMART goal need to

WORKSHEET 8.3 No Choice/Guided Choice/Free Choice

School _____

No Choice—Must Implement	Guided Choice—Must Implement Selected Aspects (select)	Free Choice (add)

WORKSHEET 8.4 Questions to Guide Selection of Focus Areas

Based on this data, what are your greatest strengths?

Based on this data what are your greatest needs?

Is the data consistent with your experience and expertise?

Is the data consistent with research findings?

What does your data tell you?

What does it not tell you?

What else do you need to know?

Based on this data, should this focus area be a priority for implementation? Why or why not?

Figure 8.4 EDMS Planning to Smart Goals: ELA

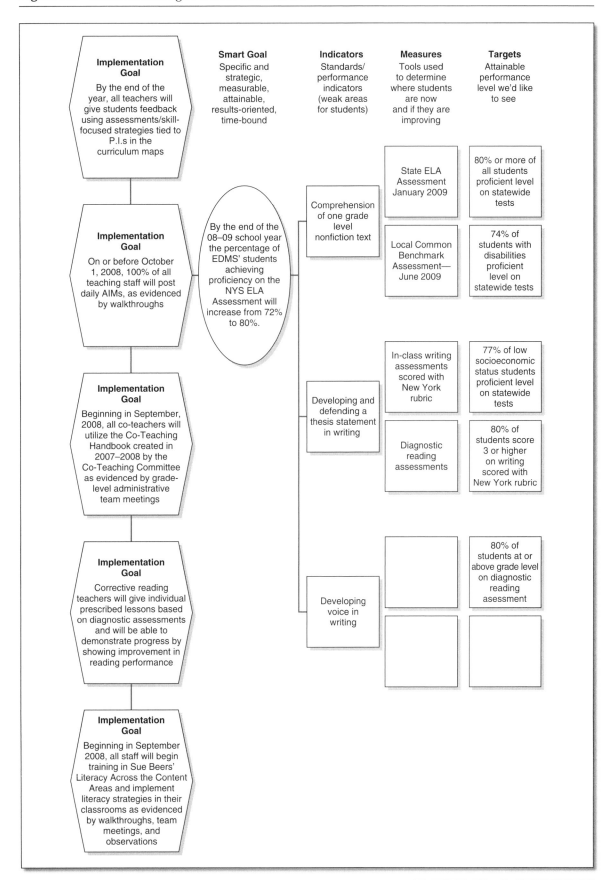

Adapted with permission from Ernie Davis Middle School, Elmira, NY, July 2008.

WORKSHEET 8.5 Planning to SMART Goals Template

Smart Goal

Specific and strategic, measurable, attainable, results-oriented, time-bound

Indicators

Standards/performance indicators (weak areas for students)

Measures

Tools used to determine where students are now and if they are improving

Targets

Attainable performance level we'd like to see

Implementation Goal

Implementation Goal

Implementation Goal

Source: O'Neill, J. (2000). SMART goals, SMART schools. *Educational Leadership*. Quality Leadership by Design, LLC

WORKSHEET 8.6 Implementation Goals Template

Given your school's SMART goals and associated targets, which essential strategies will you take to full implementation in all classrooms in the coming school year to assure the SMART goals are met? How will you document that the practices are being used routinely? What are your implementation goals?

be added. In the example shown in Figure 8.4, the implementation goals for objectives and feedback and for designating the aim are implementation goals that also support a different SMART goal in the area of mathematics and come from the *no choice* area of the district's priorities shown in the example in Figure 8.3 earlier in this chapter. By using Worksheet 8.6 to record all implementation goals, these do not have to be written over and over again in relation to different SMART goals. Having them together in one place also helps to make them a focus, keeps them at the center of awareness of those carrying out the implementation, and makes them easily accessible for strategic planning for implementation.

STEP 6: DEVELOPING THE IMPLEMENTATION PLAN

You now have completed the first two components of the implementation plan, SMART Goals and implementation goals. You are now ready to attack the processes necessary to support the desired learning results by taking the implementation goals to routine use, that is, full implementation in all classrooms, throughout the school.

As you plan for each implementation goal, consider these questions: What will you plan for those new to the district? How about the teacher who is "stuck" at mechanical use? Then there are those already implementing desired practices with fidelity before the year starts. How do you plan so that all of their needs will be met?

Similarly, you will need to plan for developmental differences in the support provided by supervisors, coaches, and mentors. All of these groups should be represented in the implementation planning process.

Worksheet 8.7 provides a planning template for process planning. The form includes the three components of implementation and space to define essential tasks, persons responsible, and dates. Make as many copies as you need to complete your plan. Your completed plan will include the following components in this order:

- Planning to SMART goals (Worksheet 8.5)
- Implementation goals (Worksheet 8.6)
- Strategic planning for implementation (Worksheet 8.7)

STEP 7: COMMUNICATING THE PLAN

In a final step in implementation planning, you will prepare for communication. It will be essential to communicate your plan early and often to all impacted.

Worksheet 8.8 provides a template for developing your communication plan. Your goals in communication are fourfold:

- To build ownership across the organization
- To promote shared learning
- To dissipate any sense of threat
- To encourage networking and seeking additional assistance

As in the entire planning process, you will want to consider multiple ways to convey your plan, considering the developmental needs of those on the receiving end. You will also want to consider the timing of the initial message, the frequency of repetition, the best persons to convey the message in different contexts and different audience, and so forth.

Having developed your implementation plan, you are ready to turn your attention to specific strategies to support implementation presented in Chapter 9. You will want to return to the implementation plan you have drafted and consider revisions you may wish to make based on your learning in Chapter 9. You may also wish to return to the plan once you have explored the information on program evaluation in the final chapter of this book.

WORKSHEET 8.7 Strategic Planning for Implementation

How will your implementation goals and SMART goals be accomplished? What essential tasks need to be carried out during the school year? What are the next steps? Who is responsible? What is the time frame?

Implementation Goal(s)	Essential Tasks	Person(s) Responsible	Dates

WORKSHEET 8.8 Communication Planning

1. How and what will you communicate with your building planning team, with the entire faculty, with students, with parents, and with other community participants in order to accomplish the following?

- Build ownership

- Promote shared learning

- Dissipate any sense of threat

- Encourage networking and seeking additional assistance

2. In what format and to whom will you present your plan?

3. How will you communicate and monitor responsibilities for ongoing data collection and analysis?

Three Strategies to Support Implementation

The implementation process transforms the curriculum from written K–12 guidelines to classroom practice. Too often, once the curriculum guide has been developed, there is a tendency for curriculum leaders to make one of three errors: (1) enjoying a well-earned rest, (2) rushing headlong into the next curriculum project, or (3) doing a good job of supporting early implementation (e.g., awareness, logistics, and resources), then moving on much too soon. In fact, the most challenging part of curriculum work is implementation. It is this phase that moves curriculum work from being an academic exercise to becoming a force for educational change.

This chapter focuses on supporting deep implementation of the curriculum through three key strategies: professional development, developmental supervision, and colleague support. The chapter also connects the concerns-based adoption model (Hord, Rutherford, Huling-Austin, & Hall, 1987) to each of the three strategies. Strategies supporting the implementation plan include building professional learning communities, data-driven decision making, selection and use of materials and resources, supervision and evaluation, pacing, and program evaluation (which is the focus of Chapter 10).

PROFESSIONAL DEVELOPMENT

The purpose of professional development is to prepare and support educators to help all students achieve high standards of learning and development.

To this end, Reeves (2005) suggests three overarching requirements for professional development:

- It must be focused on student achievement.
- It must meet the needs of individual teachers.
- It must be evaluated based on its impact on teachers, leaders, and students.

While these requirements may seem obvious, they are frequently violated in practice. For example, professional development often is evaluated based on the popularity of the presenter. Professional development calendars and schedules often reflect a "cookie cutter" approach with all staff members receiving the same information in the same way, regardless of experience and prior knowledge. Professional development offerings are not scrutinized as to research-based claims for learner impact. Even more rarely do schools or districts follow up with study of impact in their own classrooms.

The tools and examples in this chapter and the planning process described in Chapter 8 provide the wherewithal to build powerful professional development into implementation planning in your setting. Moreover, professional development, supervision, and colleague support will be planned together, yielding a robust, comprehensive approach to implementation.

Standards for Professional Development

The National Staff Development's Council's *Standards for Staff Development* were first developed in 1995 and revised in 2001. The standards are divided into three sets: context standards, process standards, and content standards. Each set is prefaced by a clear commitment to focusing professional development on student achievement: "Staff development that improves the learning of all students."

The NSDC Web site (www.nsdc.org) provides detailed discussion of each of the 12 standards, including description, rationale, and annotated bibliography. The authors strongly recommend that you and your colleagues visit that site and familiarize yourselves with its contents. The following

Figure 9.1   NSDC Standards for Professional Development (Revised, 2001)

Context Standards

Staff development that improves the learning of all students:

- Organizes adults into learning communities whose goals are aligned with those of the school and district (www.nsdc.org/standards/learningcommunities.cfm).
- Requires skillful school and district leaders who guide continuous instructional improvement (www.nsdc.org/standards/leadership.cfm).
- Requires resources to support adult learning and collaboration (www.nsdc.org/standards/resources.cfm).

Process Standards

Staff development that improves the learning of all students:

- Uses disaggregated student data to determine adult learning priorities, monitor progress, and help sustain continuous improvement (www.nsdc.org/standards/datadriven.cfm).
- Uses multiple sources of information to guide improvement and demonstrate its impact (www.nsdc.org/standards/evaluation.cfm).
- Prepares educators to apply research to decision making (www.nsdc.org/standards/researchbased.cfm).
- Uses learning strategies appropriate to the intended goal (www.nsdc.org/standards/strategies.cfm).
- Applies knowledge about human learning and change (www.nsdc.org/standards/learning.cfm).
- Provides educators with the knowledge and skills to collaborate (www.nsdc.org/standards/collaborationskills.cfm).

Content Standards

Staff development that improves the learning of all students:

- Prepares educators to understand and appreciate all students, create safe, orderly and supportive learning environments, and hold high expectations for their academic achievement (www.nsdc.org/standards/equity.cfm).
- Deepens educators' content knowledge, provides them with research-based instructional strategies to assist students in meeting rigorous academic standards, and prepares them to use various types of classroom assessments appropriately (www.nsdc.org/standards/quality.cfm).
- Provides educators with knowledge and skills to involve families and other stakeholders appropriately (www.nsdc.org/standards/family.cfm).

Source: National Staff Development Council (2001), Oxford, OH

one-hour jigsaw process is a good way to begin that process with school staff, a leadership team, or implementation planning group.

1. Have the group form subgroups of three persons each.

2. Each person in the subgroup is assigned one context standard, two process standards, and one content standard.

3. Each person has 20 minutes to prepare to discuss the rationale for each of the four assigned standards.

4. Each person has 12 minutes (3 minutes per standard) to present key points to colleagues.

The NSDC standards can be utilized in several ways to support professional development:

- The standards may be utilized to identify strengths and areas of priority need, both for specific initiatives and for the professional development program overall.
- They may be used as part of the process of evaluating the impact of professional development.
- They may be used in planning for implementation as described in Chapter 8.

The Standards and Needs Assessment

A sample standards-based needs assessment tool for the overall professional development program is included as Worksheet 9.1.

The needs assessment process helps to set priorities for learning by defining the level of current practice, identifying magnitude of need, and targeting gaps that require immediate attention. Needs assessment also provides opportunities to build on strengths and provides a process for monitoring successful implementation of professional development.

Evaluation of Offerings and the NSDC Standards

Figure 9.2 represents an evaluation form used for specific professional development activities. It illustrates, unlike in needs assessment, an individual activity is not evaluated directly in relation to each of the 12 standards. However, the prompts in the evaluation form are aligned with best practice as defined by the standards. Note that the evaluation incorporates the three types of standards: context (learning environment and resources), process (differentiation and learning experiences), and content (knowledge and modeling by presenter). Note also the direct ties to student performance.

Individual activity evaluations can be analyzed for rigor, relevance, and relationships. They also can be supplemented with other data collection. For example, Middletown's Professional Development Committee follows selected offerings with structured interviews of randomly selected participants. Interview questions are developed based on the information obtained in the activity evaluations.

A Professional Development Model

The model developed by Joyce and Showers (2002) focuses on moving staff from awareness to routine use. The professional development sequence includes information sharing, modeling, practice and feedback, and coaching. Opportunities for individuals are determined by their expressed stages of concern and their implementation of the innovation in the classroom. This model can be used in conjunction with Worksheet 9.2, later in this chapter, to plan for differentiated professional development at the school or district level.

WORKSHEET 9.1 Using NSDC Standards for Needs Assessment: Professional Development

Standard	To what extent does our professional development program reflect this Standard?	How important is this Standard to supporting learning for all students?	What is the gap?
Learning communities	1—2—3—4—5—6	1—2—3—4—5—6	
Leadership	1—2—3—4—5—6	1—2—3—4—5—6	
Resources	1—2—3—4—5—6	1—2—3—4—5—6	
Data driven	1—2—3—4—5—6	1—2—3—4—5—6	
Evaluation	1—2—3—4—5—6	1—2—3—4—5—6	
Research-based	1—2—3—4—5—6	1—2—3—4—5—6	
Design	1—2—3—4—5—6	1—2—3—4—5—6	
Learning	1—2—3—4—5—6	1—2—3—4—5—6	
Collaboration	1—2—3—4—5—6	1—2—3—4—5—6	
Equity	1—2—3—4—5—6	1—2—3—4—5—6	
Quality teaching	1—2—3—4—5—6	1—2—3—4—5—6	
Family involvement	1—2—3—4—5—6	1—2—3—4—5—6	

Source: Center for Curriculum Renewal (www.curriculumrenewal.com). Used with permission.

Note: On this scale, 1 is low and 6 is high.

Figure 9.2 Middletown City Schools—Professional Development Evaluation

Professional Development Title: _____

Date: _____

Instructor/Facilitator: _____

Please rate the following statements on the Scantron sheet.

		Strongly Agree	Agree	Disagree	Strongly Disagree	Not Applicable
1	This activity addressed topics relevant to my professional role and/or level of expertise.	A	B	C	D	E
2	The activity provided knowledge and skills that will be implemented in my teaching/professional role.	A	B	C	D	E
3	Experiences provided modeled the objectives, content, and philosophy of the activity.	A	B	C	D	E
4	The resources/materials provided were informative, practical, and useful.	A	B	C	D	E
5	The implementation of the knowledge and skills learned in this activity can have a direct impact on improving student performance.	A	B	C	D	E
6	The instructor was clear with course objectives, instructions, and presentation of information.	A	B	C	D	E
7	The instructor demonstrated a strong knowledge of content.	A	B	C	D	E
8	The instructor used effective strategies to instruct the course.	A	B	C	D	E
9	Adequate opportunities were provided for exchange of ideas with the instructor while maintaining the focus of the activity.	A	B	C	D	E
10	The instructor provided a positive learning environment.	A	B	C	D	E
11	Is district/school support needed for successful implementation of this new learning? If no, please proceed to number 13.	A (Yes)	B (No)	N/A	N/A	N/A
12	If so, please indicate below what type of support you will need:	A (Time for Planning)	B (Additional training)	C (Coaching)	D (Resources [materials, technology, etc.])	Comments (Please see below)

12. Continued:

13. General Comments:

Source: Enlarged City School District of Middletown, NY. Used with permission.

COMPREHENSIVE GOALS FOR PROFESSIONAL LEARNING

The set of comprehensive goals in Figure 9.3 was developed collaboratively by the authors and the Oswego (NY) City School District. In this case, the goals were developed explicitly to support standards-based practice. The comprehensive set of goals defines a universe of content and skills related to implementation of standards-based curriculum, instruction, and assessment. Not everything would be addressed at one time.

Goals will be set at multiple levels in the implementation process. As was discussed in Chapter 8, SMART goals are clearly tied to student results and supported by implementation goals in annual goal-setting at the building and district levels. Within each building, these goals will be implemented and personalized by learning teams and individuals. The comprehensive goals provide a framework for tracking progress over time and making certain that key elements are not ignored or forgotten. The concerns-based adoption model can be used in conjunction with this set of identified knowledge and skills to provide a valuable resource for differentiating professional development based on individual need.

THE CONCERNS-BASED ADOPTION MODEL

The concerns-based adoption model (CBAM) was initially developed at the University of Texas in the mid-1980's (Hord, Rutherford, Huling-Austin, & Hall, 1987). It provides a developmental model to support the needs of individuals in the change process. Though CBAM has multiple facets, this chapter focuses on two that are very valuable in planning professional development: stages of concern and the levels of use. Figure 9.4 shows typical levels of concern teachers have about innovations they are asked to undertake.

STAGES OF CONCERN

The stages of concern incorporated in CBAM yield important information for planning for implementation, for differentiating learning experiences, and for evaluation of the implementation process (see Chapter 8). The stages of concern evolve in a predictable way (Loucks-Horsley, 1996) and can be determined by the kinds of questions that learners ask and by the kinds of information and support they seek out on their own.

The lowest three stages of concern focus on the individual.

At Stage 0 there is no concern, or at least no immediate concern. This may be true because of lack of awareness ("I don't know that we are considering writing across the curriculum"); a lack of perceived personal relevance ("Writing belongs to the English department"); competing priorities ("As a new teacher, I have many more immediate concerns; I can't deal with this right now"); or a lack of urgency ("If I keep my head down, it will go away").

Stage 1 implementers need information as to what the innovation is ("What are the six key strategies for teaching vocabulary?") and how it works ("How does the SmartBoard work?").

Once participants have basic information, their concerns turn to personal impact. At Stage 2, they ask questions such as "Where will I find time to do this?" "How will it impact the way I grade my students?" "What's my plan to begin this work in my classroom?"

It is essential that implementation plans consider the time and effort needed to support implementers in the first three stages. If the innovation is relatively minor, if the content and concepts are relatively easy to grasp and implement, and if the staff is veteran and used to assimilating change, the time spent at these stages may be minimal. More far-reaching, complex changes will require more time and effort at Stages 0, 1, and 2.

Figure 9.3 Goals for Professional Learning in a Standards-Based System

Standards and Associated Resources

Having familiarity with standards

Understanding the role and impact of standards on teaching and learning

Using technology to access standards and related resources

Standards-Based Curricular Design

Using a standards-based curriculum for all students that is rigorous, challenging, and relevant

Selecting which standards will focus instruction

Knowing the content and skills that support the standards

Designing standards-based lessons

Designing standards-based units of study

Selecting classroom materials (textbooks, tradebooks, videos, software, etc.) to enhance student learning in relation to standards

Making strong connections within and across standards

Using technology to create standards-based units and lessons

Creating an effective year-round plan for teaching and assessing the standards for which one is responsible

Instruction for Attainment of Standards

Using strategies for brain-based learning

Providing access for all students to the knowledge and skills described in the standards

Providing equitable and prompt access for all students to accurate materials and current resources appropriate for learning goals related to the standards

Providing instruction that uses time effectively and flexibly to achieve student goals related to the standards

Engaging students in active learning, building on prior knowledge and experiences, and developing conceptual and procedural understanding, along with student independence

Using projects and assignments that require students to integrate and apply their learning in meaningful contexts and to reflect on what they have learned

Adapting the learning environment so that all students will attain the standards

Using technology to support instruction

Standards-Based Assessment, Grading, and Reporting

Designing effective systems for monitoring, assessing, and reporting student progress and success in achieving the standards

Using multiple classroom products and performances to give students feedback about their learning in relation to standards

Selecting and creating scoring guides (rubrics, checklists, answer keys) based on standards

Having students use clear criteria and examples to assess their own work

Using valid and reliable assessment tools to make decisions about student learning in relation to standards

Using assessment data to improve instruction

Employing an effective system for selecting exemplars of student work in relation to standards

Using technology to assess and report on student learning

Using strategies appropriate for standards-based grading

Reporting on student learning in relation to standards

Reporting results to the community

Working With Colleagues and Others to Implement Standards

Mentoring new teachers

Observing and giving feedback to colleagues on their practices

Using guidelines to collaboratively examine student work

Engaging in study groups on topics related to standards-based reform

Working in departments, teams, and committees

Taking a leadership role in departments, teams, and committees

Helping families and the community to support children's learning in relation to standards

Working with school and district leadership to implement standards

Using technology to communicate with colleagues about standards-based curriculum, instruction, and assessment

Source: Oswego City School District, NY and Center for Curriculum Renewal (www.curriculumrenewal.com). Used with permission.

Figure 9.4 Typical Expressions of Concern About an Innovation

Stage of Concern		Expression of Concern
"Impact"	6.	I have some ideas about something that would work even better.
	5.	I would like to coordinate my effort with others, to maximize the innovation's effect.
	4.	How is my use affecting learners? How can I refine it to have more impact?
"Task"	3.	I seem to be spending all my time getting materials ready.
"Self"	2.	How will using it affect me?
	1.	I would like to know more about it.
"Unconcerned"	0.	I am not concerned about it.

Source: George, Hall, & Stiegelbauer, 2008, p. 4. Reprinted with permission of SEDL. Copyright © 2006, SEDL.

The middle stage, management, begins at the earliest stage of implementation. Without strong support at Stage 3, many users will never progress beyond the management of the program in the classroom (albeit that they may become much better at it over time). As far as implementation, Stage 3 requires careful attention to establishing norms of use in terms of student management, time management, unit and lesson planning, and assessment and reporting.

At the highest stages of concern, the focus shifts to results. At Stage 4, implementers ask questions related to the performance of their students and use student data to refine their practice in the classroom. Often Stage 4 implementers seek out others of like mind to compare notes, share successes and failures, and learn together. This leads to Stage 5, collaboration, which is the ultimate goal for implementation.

Some implementers will move to Stage 6, committing themselves to seek ways to fine tune and improve the innovation. This often occurs as a result of collaboration efforts emerging at Stage 5.

If individuals' needs are met at a given stage of concern, it is likely that they will ratchet practice to the next stage. If not, they may well remain "stuck" at lower levels than potential and importance warrant. This, then, impacts the teacher's level of use (LoU) of the innovation, as shown in Figure 9.5.

LEVELS OF USE

The stages of concern in CBAM tie directly to levels of use. Combining the questions the implementer is asking with what that teacher is actually doing in the classroom provides strong evidence for the efficacy of implementation.

The first, and in some ways most critical, implementation goal is to support all staff to move from mechanical to routine use. At that point, the staff members will have established routines, procedures, and teaching practices to effectively implement the innovation. As important is that at the routine use level they will have begun to ask and answer questions related to the successful performance of their students.

Once teachers move from mechanical to routine use, attention can shift to the second implementation goal: to support staff members as they collaborate to improve results and seek ways to improve the innovation.

Figure 9.5 LoU in the Field

LoU 0	**Nonuse:** When asked, Mary states that she does not know anything about interim assessments. She has not talked to anyone about it/them and has no plans to do so. Yes, it was mentioned at a faculty meeting but she didn't pay attention.
LoU I	**Orientation:** Jose attended a workshop on the importance of using interim assessments. He has not decided to include interim assessments in his teaching, but is thinking about it. He has talked with his department chair and one of his colleagues.
LoU II	**Preparation:** In Betsey's school the principal has decided that all teachers will do interim assessments. Betsey has bought two books about interim assessments and found several useful sites on the Web. These sites have provided several assessments that she thinks she can use. They have helped her prepare to start using interim assessments next term.
LoU III	**Mechanical Use:** Greg is spending at least two hours every weekend developing interim assessments to use in the coming week. Some of the assessments have worked, but several have been confusing to his students. He has had to rework those plus build the new ones for the subsequent week. He also developed some that he never had time to use.
LoU IVA	**Routine Use:** Adele is using interim assessments the same way this year as she did last year. She has a bank of them and can pull out the most appropriate ones to use as she goes along. She sees them as important to knowing what her students understand, She finds her assessments correlate well with how her students do on the state tests.
LoU IVB	**Refinement:** Jeff has compiled the data from the assessments that he used last term. He sees that some of his students consistently perform lower, but he believes they really have learned the material. As he has checked into it, he sees a pattern: those students who do not read well are not performing well on his interim assessments. He now is going to try to develop some assessments that do not rely on reading.
LoU V	**Integration:** In the fall Fran and Joan decided to use the same interim assessments with their freshman English classes. They are now able to compare how well students are learning the benchmarks. Fran's students were not doing as well as Joan's in two areas. So this term she is using Joan's lesson plans to see if her students will do better.
LoU VI	**Renewal:** Chancellor has used interim assessments and found that they really help with student understanding and his knowing how each student is progressing. Now he is looking into a computerized system that will administer the tests, keep each student's records, and compile a class profile.

AN EXAMPLE LINKING CBAM AND PROFESSIONAL DEVELOPMENT

Kate Fenton, Director of Professional Development in the Springfield, Massachusetts Public Schools, has combined and linked teacher concerns with potential options for professional development. We have adapted Fenton's work in Worksheet 9.2.

Note that for this purpose we have limited the levels of concern to these four: awareness, management, routine use, and renewal. At each of these four levels, there are multiple options for professional development listed. These options, and others that you may add, can be used to differentiate professional development for your teachers based on the concerns they are expressing. The tool can also be used to track changes in concerns over time.

WORKSHEET 9.2 Professional Development: Matching Approaches to Concerns

Review the typical teacher concerns at each level: Awareness, Management, Routine Use, and Renewal in Column 1.

Discuss examples of questions and concerns you are hearing from your teachers and record them at the appropriate level. Based on this data, select approaches to differentiating professional development for your teachers. Use the approaches in Column 3 as guidelines but feel free to add approaches to fit your needs.

	Typical Teacher Concerns	Concerns Expressed by Our Teachers	Approaches to Consider
Renewal	• How the practice is affecting student achievement • How they can employ the practice more effectively		• Teachers evaluate its use • Teachers set up system for student assessment • Teachers generate manuals and resource guides • Experienced teachers serve as mentors • How the practice is affecting student achievement • How they can employ the practice more effectively
Routine Use	• Why it works sometimes and not others • If they are doing it effectively • Their ability to teach it to others		• Set up coaching situations • Opportunities for professional sharing and reflection • Teachers set agendas for reflection meetings • Teachers conduct workshops for other teachers
Management	• Why it is taking so much time and effort • Why it doesn't go as smoothly in classrooms as it does in workshops		• Focused sessions with hands-on materials teachers will use with students • Opportunities for practice in context to debug practice • Reflection and discussion • Feedback from peers • Feedback from teachers experienced with the practice • Teachers observe the practice in use • Intervisitations • Discuss the connection between theory and practice
Awareness	• How it works • What it looks like in practice • Materials and time required • Availability of support • If it will help them • If it will help their students		• Teachers share experiences • Teachers share prior/common knowledge • Teachers experienced with practice share • Students who have used the practice share • Form focus groups to study the new practice • All for question and answer • Provide theoretical framework

Adapted from Kate Fenton, Springfield (MA) Public Schools, n.d. Used with permission.

Figure 9.6 was developed by the authors to link three key support structures to Fenton's four levels. These include a developmental supervision model by Glickman, Gordon, and Ross-Gordon (2007), the professional development model developed by Joyce and Showers (2002), and a continuum of mentoring, coaching, and colleague support.

Figure 9.6   Matching Concerns to Support Strategies

Concern Level	Support Strategies		
	Developmental supervision (Glickman, 2007)	Professional development (Joyce & Showers, 2002)	Colleague support (Carr, Harris, & Herman, 2005)
Renewal	Nondirective		Collaboration
Routine Use	Collaborative/nondirective	Structured feedback, coaching	Coaching
Management	Directive informational/ collaborative	Initial practice, structured feedback	Mentoring and coaching
Management		Demonstration and modeling	
Awareness	Directive informational	Description and theory	Mentoring and coaching
Awareness	Directive control		

Source: Center for Curriculum Renewal (www.curriculumrenewal.com). Used with permission.

LINKING CONCERNS TO SUPERVISION—GLICKMAN'S DEVELOPMENTAL SUPERVISION MODEL

Carl Glickman and colleagues (2007) have developed an invaluable developmental approach to supervision that works quite well in concert with CBAM. Glickman's model incorporates four approaches to supervision, defined by the roles and responsibilities of the teacher and supervisor.

The *directive control* approach is utilized when the teacher lacks the awareness, skills, or will to approach the innovation. It is also used when the innovation is of critical importance to the school or district but not to the teacher. Rarely utilized in the school setting, it may be used when there is not time to collaborate or when circumstances require immediate, unilateral decisions.

In CBAM terms, directive control is used to move staff members from awareness to an informational level, or from nonuse to orientation.

The directive control approach places the locus of control squarely at the supervisor level. While the supervisor may engage the teacher in discussion of the problem, the supervisor determines the solution and communicates expectations directly and unequivocally to the teacher. The supervisor also takes primary responsibility for closely monitoring progress of the teacher both in professional development and in implementation.

The *directive informational* approach works well when the teacher has the interest and the will, but not the expertise, to embrace the innovation. The teacher may not know what he or she doesn't know or may be acutely aware of confusion and inexperience. The teacher may have experienced failure in implementation because of attempting to implement without the foundational prerequisites to succeed or may be putting off implementation.

In CBAM terms, the teacher's concerns often will reflect the need for information and personal understanding, as well as the need to see the innovation modeled in the classroom.

As with the directive control approach, the supervisor utilizing directive informational supervision will retain the locus of control. In this instance, the supervisor is more likely to present choices to the teacher, so long as the supervisor believes that any of the choices can have the desired effect on teacher awareness and performance.

The directive control and directive informational approaches are preferred professional development approaches at the awareness level. Collaborative supervision is introduced as the teacher moves through management and into routine use and continues to be the approach as the teacher pays greater attention to student results, refines practice, and assimilates the innovation into practice.

Collaborative supervision requires active listening by both the supervisor and teacher as they come to understand one another's perceptions and priorities and jointly develop a plan for implementation and support. As attention shifts to increased focus on student results, the teacher and supervisor come to jointly share accountability for those results and therefore become increasingly invested in the success of the innovation.

As the teacher's concerns reflect efforts to refocus, improve, and innovate (moving into the renewal level), a combination of collaborative and nondirective supervision may be indicated. The role of the supervisor is to facilitate and support the teachers or teams as they determine their own priorities. Despite the "nondirective" label, the supervisor is very involved from a support perspective.

When incorporating developmental supervision in planning for implementation, it is important to remember that not only will different individuals require different supervisory behaviors, but also that selection of approach for each individual will fluctuate according to experience, expertise, and interest. The same teacher may be an expert in reading strategies, an interested novice in implementing a new mathematics curriculum, and indifferent as to a new approach to student management. In each case, the supervisory approach and the professional development for that teacher will look quite different.

DIFFERENTIATING CONVERSATIONS WITH HIGH-, MIDDLE- AND LOW-PERFORMING TEACHERS

Quint Studer (2008) has described three very different conversations effective leaders need to initiate with high, middle, and low performers in organizations.

The best teachers must be recognized, reinforced, and supported. Middle-performing teachers must be acknowledged for their good work and helped to set a clear goal for improvement. Low-performing teachers must be made aware of one area of unacceptable performance, told what performance is expected, and informed what the consequence will be if the expected performance is not attained. The following are examples of conversations between a principal and teachers at each performance level.

A Sample Conversation With a High-Performing Teacher

Shelley, Edison High School is well on our way to being the top high school in the county, and one of the nation's top 100 high schools. As you know our student results are now 3rd in the county, as compared to 11th three years ago. We continue to invest in ways to increase

Figure 9.7 Differentiating Conversations With High, Middle, and Low Performers

High	Middle	Low
Tell them where the school and district are going.	Tell why they are so important to the school and district.	Describe the issue that has been observed.
Thank them for their work.	Share one area for development and improvement.	Describe how disappointed you feel.
Outline why they are so important.	End with a statement of support.	Describe specifically what needs to be done.
Ask whether there is anything you can do for them.		Describe consequences of continued low performance.

Adapted from Studer, Q. (2008) *Results That Last: Hardwiring Behaviors That Will Take Your Company to the Top*

performance in our special education and English language learners subgroups and also ways to increase rigor and challenge for our top students.

I want to thank you for your key role in our school. Your work in developing common assessments for all levels of English classes has already made a huge impact in promoting consistent, high expectations. I am also very aware that your students outperform the school and state averages in all subgroups and that you have the most students performing at the highest level of any teacher in the school.

Thanks specifically for your work in mentoring four new English teachers in the past three years. All four teachers are already producing strong student performance results and two have begun to assume leadership roles in the organization.

What more can I do to support you in your work? What ways can I be of help?

A Sample Conversation With a Middle-Performing Teacher

Tim, your work in promoting instructional use of Smartboards in our classrooms is making a huge difference. Your development of the 10 hours awareness session required of all teachers and your in-classroom support of teachers having technical difficulties are two major reasons that teachers are beginning to use this technology in the classroom.

Now that most of the introductory sessions are complete I would like you to focus on building and supporting a high end users group in the school. I want you to identify teachers with high potential and bring them together for advanced coaching and support. I want these teachers to not only significantly change the learning experiences for their students but also to raise the bar for their colleagues.

Thanks again, Tim, for the work you are doing. What more can I do to support you in this important work ahead?

A Sample Conversation With A Low-Performing Teacher

Joyce, as you are well aware, in your two sections of Advanced Placement biology, not a single one of the 34 students scored at level three or four. Twenty-eight of the same students took one or more other AP courses, and these students attained level three or four 73% of the time.

You know that our school has made a commitment to increased rigor for our strongest students. Not only do we expect that, but the parents and community expect it as well. Our Advanced Placement performance has increased substantially in every subject area but one. I am disappointed that it is your students who have not kept pace.

I want you to work with your department chair and me to complete a gap analysis of your Advanced Placement results for the past three years. Once we find out where your students are underperforming, I expect you to meet with your department chair and me weekly to review your instruction and review the assessments you are using in your classroom.

Joyce, if your results do not improve in the spring semester, you will not teach Advanced Placement students next year.

Studer (2008) has found that on average 92% of employees are performing at middle and high levels. He recommends that conversations like those above need to happen with all employees so that everyone knows where they stand. These conversations should happen first with high performers, then middle performers, and then low performers.

In concluding this discussion of supervision, we turn to the importance of what Schmoker (2006) refers to as our "positive deviants." He reminds us that the most powerful way to drive instructional change is to provide organized opportunities for teachers to learn from the best of their own, then from one another. Internal support is more trusted, is more readily available, and often met with less resistance. These "positive deviants" operate at the "renewal" level of concern and the high end of Studer's performance levels and are often willing and even eager to lead if asked and supported.

MENTORING, COACHING, AND COLLABORATION

The third key strategy for supporting implementation includes mentoring, coaching, and collaboration. Although these overlap in practice in our work and writing, we distinguish them as follows (Carr et al., 2005):

- Mentorship as experienced professionals working with colleagues new to the profession or new to the district
- Coaching of two types: peer coaching focused on instructional improvement and professional growth, and leadership coaching to assist both new and veteran leaders in leading implementation, building learning communities in their schools and leadership teams, and professional growth
- Collaboration in contexts such as study groups, data teams, curriculum committees, grade-level teams, and departments

Mentors and coaches can make very effective use of the developmental supervision continuum described above, although they play supportive rather than supervisory roles. Mentors generally spend much of their time utilizing directive informational techniques, especially in support of the induction process. They also collaborate, often in the form of providing structured feedback. The coaching process is largely collaborative, although the coach may also play a directive informational role as experienced professionals work to assimilate new learning. An effective coach can also play a significant role in the continued growth of a professional at the refocusing stage and renewal level.

Collaboration requires participants to take shared responsibility for setting goals and targets, for determining operating procedures, and for gathering, analyzing, and using results.

IMPLICATIONS FOR IMPLEMENTATION PLANNING

The previous chapter described a comprehensive planning process for supporting implementation, incorporating professional development, supervision, and colleague support. Return now to the plans you began in that chapter and consider these questions:

1. What concerns are your teachers and administrators expressing about the innovations you have identified in your implementation goals? What does this tell you about their stages of concern?

2. What ways will you track what is actually happening in the classroom to monitor levels of use?

3. Does your implementation plan reflect the sequence of information and support inherent in CBAM?

4. Does your implementation plan anticipate the need for differentiated professional development based on the experience, expertise, and commitment of your staff?

5. How will you continue to use the stages of concern and levels of use to modify your implementation plan over time?

The next chapter expands on these types of considerations as you turn your attention to program evaluation.

10

Curriculum-Based Program Evaluation

"Evaluate our programs? Our test scores tell us all we need to know."

"Curriculum evaluation—sounds like someone's out to bash teachers again!"

"Who has the time? It's hard enough to find time to teach the curriculum."

"Evaluate our curriculum? Makes sense, but I don't know the first thing about it. I'm a teacher, not a number cruncher."

"We do program evaluation. Every 10 years a team comes in and tells us how we're doing."

These responses, and others like them, frequently follow a proposal to evaluate the curriculum. Most educators are very aware of the pressures of accountability systems based on high stakes testing, adequate yearly progress and public school report. Fewer educators come from the "cardiac" school of assessment—in our hearts, we know we're wonderful—than was the case a generation ago. Yet many have not experienced the power of meaningful curriculum-based program evaluations beyond test results and possibly external audits such as those conducted by accrediting agencies such as the Middle States Association of Colleges and Schools. Others may lack a conceptual framework for the task and may wrongly assume that evaluation at the programmatic level is beyond their ken.

This chapter provides an introduction to curriculum-based program evaluation to the end of achieving the following outcomes:

- To develop a common language and knowledge base related to program evaluation
- To provide a practical working model for planning, designing, and implementing program evaluation
- To provide tools for managing the process
- To ensure that program evaluation supports learning and teaching; in other words, that the process links directly with the implementation of the curriculum in the classroom

This overview provides useful, practical information for program evaluation and may spark interest in further pursuing technical issues of design, theory, validity, and reliability, and the many other complexities of program evaluation that are beyond the scope of this book. However, while good assessment practice at the school and district levels does emphasize data-driven decision making, it also can and does emanate from experience and plain common sense. This chapter helps to frame practical evaluation processes to lead to sensible curriculum implementation and revision.

In this chapter, we consider planning the program evaluation, including

- Establishing the purpose
- Developing the logic model
- Identifying key questions
- Selecting data sources and data analysis
- Reporting results

WHAT IS CURRICULUM-BASED PROGRAM EVALUATION?

Curriculum-based program evaluation can be defined as a process of determining the value and effectiveness of a program for the purpose of decision making. There are several key points in this definition.

- Program evaluation is a process. It is not an instrument, a tool, or a set of data.
- Program evaluation determines worth (Is the program worth pursuing?) and merit (Is the program achieving what it set out to do?).
- Program evaluation exists for decision making, providing information for program planning, revision, and continuation.

DEFINING THE PURPOSE

In beginning the program evaluation process, it is essential to define its purpose. What decisions must be made? What information will help to make them?

In general there are two purposes for program evaluation. The first is accountability—the process provides data to inform students, teachers, administrators, parents, and the community as to how well the program is doing. The second is program improvement—the evaluation provides information that helps educators improve the program to better meet the needs of the students.

A common distinction is that between *formative* and *summative* evaluation. Formative evaluation is ongoing evaluation that results in fine tuning and reshaping the curriculum as part of the continuous process of program improvement. Summative evaluation occurs as a snapshot of program progress at a specified point in time and may be used to make accountability-related decisions as to program continuation, revision, or termination.

Remember that the same question may provide both formative and summative information. For example, the results of a reading assessment may be used formatively to group students and inform instruction. This same assessment may be used summatively to provide information as to individual and group performance and growth.

For program evaluation to succeed, you must convince several groups, each of which may be skeptical, that it is worth doing:

- Teachers must see that it will make a difference for themselves and their students—that it is not just another paper chase.
- Administrators must see that it provides useful information for the management, operation, and instructional leadership of the school.

- School board members must see that curriculum assessment helps to advance their policies and directions for the school system.

These internal groups must buy into program evaluation at the outset. Other key groups, such as parents, business organizations, and student government, may also be critical depending on the program and the situation.

DO WE NEED AN EXTERNAL EVALUATOR?

Two common but opposing errors often happen in program evaluation. The first is assuming that "hired help" can best do the entire job. In fact, if teachers and administrators don't own the evaluation, they won't use it. The opposite mistake is not to ask for outside help when it is clearly needed. Worksheet 10.1, Determining Whether an External Evaluator Is Needed, can be used to decide if an outside consultant is needed and for what purposes.

The answers to the seven questions on Worksheet 10.1 may tell you that you need to hire a consultant. If so, proceed carefully.

- Make sure you tell the consultant what is expected. Some consultants have one bag of tricks they shoehorn into any need.
- Ascertain the consultant's commitment to you and time availability. You need help when you need help, not when the consultant has spring break.
- Spell out your expectations in a written contract that is signed by the consultant and a representative of the district. Periodically review the contract to make sure it is being carried out or to make needed adjustments.

DEVELOPING THE LOGIC MODEL AND EVALUATION QUESTIONS

A logic model is "a simplified model of how activities are understood to contribute to a chain of intended outcomes and finally to the ultimate outcome that helps to plan, implement, monitor, and evaluate an intervention" (Rogers, 2007, p. 3).

In its simplest form (and the form we prefer to use) a logic model describes three components: resources and conditions, programs and practices, and student results (Carr & Harris, 2001). While more complex logic models exist (e.g., distinguishing outcomes and outputs, and describing feedback loops and multiple causal paths), we find that the basic form works well in school settings. The fundamental purposes of the logic model are

- to help us think about and articulate program theory;
- to provide a road map and visual organizer for participants and program evaluators;
- to explicitly link activities to results;
- to assure collection of data, not only about results but also about the resources and practices intended to lead to desired results;
- to organize and manage evaluation activities; and
- to organize the evaluation report.

The following series of questions describes the sections of the logic model, the resources and conditions (inputs), the programs and practices, and the results:

- *Resources and Conditions (Inputs)*—What are the human, fiscal, organizational, and community resources (materials, time, money, people, expertise, conceptual model) available to build and implement the program?

WORKSHEET 10.1 Determining Whether an External Evaluator Is Needed

As a group, the planning team should discuss the following questions and reach consensus on a response for each one. For each question, circle the response that represents your group consensus. Note: On this scale, 1 is low and 6 is high.

To What Extent . . .

1 2 3 4 5 6 7   1. Do we need an outside expert to work with our staff, board, or administration?

1 2 3 4 5 6 7   2. Are there questions that need to be asked but that are hard to ask in-house?

1 2 3 4 5 6 7   3. Will an external evaluator lend us credibility?

1 2 3 4 5 6 7   4. Do we need technical expertise in design?

1 2 3 4 5 6 7   5. Do we need technical support in data collection and analysis?

1 2 3 4 5 6 7   6. Do we need help in preparing and communicating an assessment report?

1 2 3 4 5 6 7   7. Do we have time to attend to the details of curriculum assessment?

• *Programs and Practices*—What are the processes, tools, events, technology, and actions planned for and actually delivered? What are students and teachers actually doing in classrooms? For example, while the amount of time is an input, the way time is used is a process.

• *Results*—What is the impact of the program? What do students know, value, and believe? What are they able to do? What are the specific changes in the teachers' and students' behavior, knowledge, skills, status, and levels of functioning? What fundamental intended or unintended changes occurred for students, teachers, and systems as a result of the program?

This logic model guides design of the questions that will be addressed through the evaluation. A useful way to organize program evaluation questions is by using the three-by-three matrix in Figure 10.1.

One axis of this matrix is defined by questions related to resources and conditions (inputs), programs and practices, and results. The second axis of the matrix defines whether the questions focus primarily on students, teachers, or programs. This matrix may be expanded to include parents, administrators, or others as warranted by the program.

Typically, when the program being evaluated is a curriculum area (e.g., math or science or English language arts), the focus is on student results, on the programs and practices intended to support students in attaining those results, and on the resources and conditions (inputs) necessary to implement the desired programs and practices in the classroom.

Figure 10.1 Matrix of Program Evaluation Questions

	Resources and Conditions (Inputs)	Programs and Practices	Results
Student	Is the curriculum made available to all students? (text, facilities, schedule, etc.)	Are learning experiences matched to the student and the tasks at hand? (learning styles, diagnostic assessment, etc.)	Is the student learning at an acceptable rate? Is the assessment of performance based on goals? (knowledge, skills, attitudes, appreciation)
Teacher	Does instructional planning match the curriculum? (time allocation, selection of materials, staff development, etc.)	Do instructional strategies match the student and the task at hand? (differentiated instruction, assessment, management, etc.)	Does instruction lead to changes in student performance? Does the teacher's performance meet expectations?
Program	Does the allocation of time, people, and resources match the curriculum? (budget, staffing, master schedule, etc.)	Do teaching strategies and learning activities match the curriculum? (time on task, interaction analysis, etc.)	Are the goals of the program being reached? Are they the right goals?

FOCUSING THE PROGRAM EVALUATION

The written curriculum guidelines you developed using the processes described in Chapter 5 include three sections that match the logic model and form the basis for focusing your program evaluation design.

You established curriculum *goals*. These goals established the broad concepts, skills, knowledge, and attitudes that students would exhibit as a result of completing the curriculum. These goals will become the basis for your results assessment. Results assessment establishes those areas of student performance that you deem worth measuring and reporting.

You established *instructional guidelines.* These guidelines serve to specify approaches and practices to facilitate student learning. These guidelines become the basis for practices evaluation, in which you assess student and teacher, administrator, and parent behaviors and interactions occurring in the implementation of the curriculum.

Finally, you established *needs and recommendations.* These specified materials, staff development, time, staffing, and other necessities for appropriate implementation of the curriculum. These needs and recommendations become the basis for your input and resources assessment, in which you assess the extent to which the necessary resources and conditions are provided and support implementation. Figure 10.2 illustrates this relationship.

Figure 10.2 Curriculum Development and Program Evaluation: Making the Connection

Your statement of needs and recommendations (Chapter 5), _____
_____
_____
_____

is the basis for your evaluation of input and results.

Your statement of instructional guidelines (Chapter 5), _____
_____
_____
_____

is the basis for your evaluation of practices.

Your statement of curriculum goals (Chapter 5),_____
_____
_____
_____

is the basis for your evaluation of results.

The importance of making direct connections between the written curriculum guidelines and the evaluation design cannot be overstated. Failure to do so destroys the resonance among the written, implemented, and assessed curriculum that is so essential to focused program improvement.

CREATING PROGRAM EVALUATION QUESTIONS

What is it that you wish to find out through curriculum assessment? The most meaningful evaluations are those in which information about related inputs and resources, practices, and results is collected. One type of information alone is of little use for program improvement. Suppose, for example, that a goal of the curriculum is "Students will use mathematics to solve problems in the everyday world." Through outcome assessment, you discover that students are not achieving this goal. But without information about related inputs and resources ("Have the needed manipulative materials been purchased?") and related implementation practices ("What percentage of instructional time is devoted to real-world problem solving?"), you do not know why student achievement in this area is not satisfactory. Thus you will want to include in your evaluation questions drawn directly from your needs and recommendations (input and resource questions), from your instructional guidelines (practice questions), and from your curriculum goals (results questions).

If a goal in the written curriculum guidelines is "Students will use mathematics to solve problems in the everyday world," the results question could be "Can students use mathematics to solve problems in the everyday world?" If an instructional guideline is "Students should spend the majority of their time in mathematics class involved in real-world problem-solving activities," the practices question could be "Do students spend the majority of their time in mathematics class involved in real-world problem-solving activities?" If a need is manipulative materials and the recommendation is that these be purchased for all classrooms, the input and resources question could be "What manipulative materials have been purchased?" Figure 10.3 shows additional examples of evaluation questions based directly on components from curriculum guidelines.

Use Worksheet 10.2 to practice writing evaluation questions tied directly to inputs and results, practices, and results. Use the questions in Figure 10.3 as exemplars.

Figure 10.3   Examples of Evaluation Questions

Inputs and Resources	Questions
Availability of science materials and funds must be assured	1. What science materials are currently in the inventory at each school site? 2. What is the budget for science materials and equipment at each school site? 3. How do teachers influence the ordering of science materials at each school site?
Practices	
Teachers need to provide opportunities for students to read materials written for a variety of purposes.	1. What types of materials are being read by students (e.g., at each grade level, in each subject area, in each school)?
Results	
Students will use mathematics to solve problems in the everyday world.	1. To what degree can students invent approaches to solve problems? 2. To what degree can students construct approaches to solving math problems that they encounter at home and in the work force?

SETTING PRIORITIES

Look over the questions you have listed on Worksheet 10.2. Is it possible to answer all of these questions or does the prospect of doing so seem overwhelming? Will it get done, given the time required and competing demands for time? Often program assessments that get into trouble do so not because of lack of commitment but because the task at hand is not manageable. This is the time to set priorities. It is much better to obtain good, accurate information about the most essential issues than to "shotgun" and know very little about a great deal. Which are the most essential questions, given the time, energy, and resources you can place into curriculum assessment? As you continue to identify questions to supplement those developed in Worksheet 10.2, rate the priority of each question. Then reach consensus about which are the highest priority questions. These are the questions that will form the basis of your curriculum-based program evaluation.

WORKSHEET 10.2 **Practice in Writing Program Evaluation Questions**

1. Select three needs and recommendations you created in Chapter 5. For each write an input and resources evaluation question. Repeat the process with the instructional guidelines (practices questions) and curriculum goals (results questions).

Needs and Recommendations Statement	Resources and Conditions (Inputs) Evaluation Question
1.	1.
2.	2.
3.	3.
Instructional Guidelines	Programs and Practices Questions
4.	4.
5.	5.
6.	6.
Curriculum Goals	Student Results Questions

2. With a partner exchange and critique your program evaluation questions using the following criteria:

   A. Do the questions clearly state what is to be measured? (clarity, succinctness)

   B. Do the questions actually measure the corresponding needs and recommendations, instructional guideline, or curriculum goal? (alignment)

   C. Is the question one that can actually be asked and answered in the school context? (efficacy)

   D. Will the question have value in improving learning or meeting accountability requirements? (utility)

DETERMINING DATA TO BE COLLECTED

Now you need to specify what data you need to answer each question. At this point, do not worry about how to get the data. For instance, if time spent teaching science is a high-priority input, you may decide that you need to know the minutes per week devoted to science teaching (the data). There are several ways this data could be gathered—analysis of master schedules, teacher logs, plan books, and the like. However, it is generally more efficient and effective to determine what you need to know first, then return later to selecting actual tools and analysis processes.

What is important is that the type of data collected relates directly to the assessment question the data is intended to answer. Examples of common types of conditions and resources, programs and practices, and results are shown in Figure 10.4.

You have now answered the first of two essential design questions ("What do we need to know?"), and you are ready to address the second ("How can we best get the information?").

DATA SOURCES

For each assessment question and type of data, there will be one or more possible ways to collect information. Ideally, each question will be addressed from at least two perspectives—either by using a particular data collection instrument with two different groups or by using more than one data collection instrument with any one group. Multiple data sources provide reliability and help to ensure that important information is not overlooked or misrepresented.

Any type of data source is only valuable to the degree that it is an appropriate means of answering your assessment questions. For example, paper-and-pencil tests are not appropriate to use to

Figure 10.4   Examples of Data Types

Resources and Conditions (Inputs)

Supplies, equipment, materials
Written curriculum documents
Time
Teacher preparation
Staffing
Student/staff ratio
Policies and procedures

Programs and Practices

Use of available supplies, materials, equipment
Time allocation
Student/teacher direction of activities
Implementation of policies and procedures
Teaching and learning techniques employed in the classroom

Results

Individual achievement (computation, content knowledge, etc.)
Group achievement
Attitudes (toward self, learning, school, mathematics, etc.)
Attributes (self-reliance, self-control, cooperativeness, etc.)
Behaviors (attendance, participation, etc.)
Short-term outcomes (attendance rates, graduation rates, etc.)
Long-term outcomes (employment, success in future study, etc.)

measure students' application of process skills in science but may be an efficient and appropriate means of measuring students' knowledge of math facts.

Figure 10.5 describes advantages and disadvantages of common assessment instruments. Use this information as you return to the evaluation questions you analyzed earlier, this time connecting the program evaluation questions to data sources. Note that multiple measures are used in all cases. This increases the internal validity of the program evaluation, so long as each measure is carefully designed and implemented. Figure 10.6 shows an example of connecting evaluation questions to data sources for evaluation of a literacy-across-the-curriculum program.

We now turn our attention to discussion of the logistics of gathering data and analyzing the information.

Figure 10.5   Common Assessment Instruments: Advantages and Disadvantages

Type of Assessment	Advantages	Disadvantages
Large-Scale and Standardized Assessments	• Have usually been field-tested and checked for reliability and validity • Are relatively inexpensive and easy to administer • Can provide comparison data to external populations	• May or may not address the questions that concern you • Frequently require application of knowledge in an artificial situation • May be misinterpreted and misused
Locally Developed Common Assessments	• Can be specially designed to answer your questions • Can be administered in a regular class setting • Can build local ownership in the results	• Developing valid and reliable tests is exceedingly time-consuming, costly, and difficult • May lack credibility, particularly if used exclusively
Portfolios of Student Work	• Provide cumulative records of student growth and development • Can be designed to include multiple data sources for the same question • Can be valuable instructional tools • Can be excellent sources of communication with students and parents	• Require considerable time and effort to maintain • Can become unwieldy • Require considerable staff training in collection and analysis for appropriate maintenance and use • Require clearly articulated and understood criteria for analysis if comparison is desired
Observation	• Can provide first-hand information on complex events • Particularly useful in assessing implementation	• Observers can change the environment being observed • Requires considerable investment of time and effort • Requires careful training of observers
Interviews and Focus Groups	• Allow in-depth discussion of events and issues • Can provide information difficult to obtain from other sources	• Relatively costly • Require careful training of interviewers
Surveys and Questionnaires	• Relatively inexpensive and easy to administer • Can provide a great deal of information in a short time • Easily manageable	• Require careful development and administration • Respondents may not be truthful • Limit type of information obtained • Because of ease of administration, can be overused

Figure 10.6 Example of Methodology Tied to Program Evaluation Questions

Literacy Across the Curriculum (LAC) — Data Collection Sources Checklist	Survey	Interview	Observation	Document Review	Data Analysis
Resources and Conditions (Input) Questions					
To what extent is LAC an explicit, stated goal of the school curriculum at the elementary, middle, and high school levels overall to date?				X	
Have teachers received adequate professional development in LAC implementation?	X	X	X	X	
Are there age-appropriate, student-centered materials available for instruction?	X	X	X		
Is there adequate time for teacher planning and instruction?	X	X			
Are data, literacy, or other curriculum coaches available? Are they being utilized effectively?	X	X	X		X
Programs and Practices Questions					
Are given materials used appropriately?			X		
Is instruction aligned with standards?				X	X
Is the stated curriculum being taught and assessed?				X	X
Is instruction time being used effectively?				X	X
Are modifications and adaptations provided for students with special needs?				X	X
Is differentiated instruction taking place?				X	X
Do students know what the stated learning objective is?		X			
Results Questions					
How is assessment data being used? Does it show student strengths and weaknesses?				X	X
Did specified subgroups perform adequately?					X
What is the consensus of school climate?	X	X			
To what extent is classroom assessment used to give feedback to students about their learning?	X	X	X		
Other than student achievement, how are student results being assessed?		X		X	

SURVEY DATA

Surveys provide the opportunity to gather data on a wide range of topics from a large number of stakeholders. It is also possible to gather similar data from different groups, such as teachers, parents, and administrators. Surveys are relatively inexpensive, especially if they are administered online. We highly recommend online surveys as they eliminate the need for paper and postage.

In most situations, we develop surveys that combine three types of information: demographic, quantitative, and qualitative. Demographic data, such as building assignment, years of experience, and ethnicity, allow for disaggregation of the data by subgroups.

Quantitative data is usually collected by means of a Likert scale (such as 1 through 5) on constructs such as frequency, importance, and value.

Qualitative survey data emerges from responses to open-ended questions.

Most online survey software will provide frequency summaries of Likert scale and demographic data. This is a huge time saver and is highly recommended; the cost of the survey software is quickly recouped in savings of time and effort.

INTERVIEWS

Interviews provide the opportunity to explore key evaluation questions in depth with key people involved in the program and to provide opportunities for respondents to provide information in an isolated setting. They also provide data that can be compared across interviewees to detect major themes, successes, and concerns.

In order to ensure consistency, we develop interview schedules including queries and prompts and train interviewers in their use. Figure 10.7 is an example of such an interview schedule. Note that the queries, in boldface, are asked verbatim of all interviewees. Prompts may be used, modified, or ignored based on the responses.

Focus groups have many of the advantages of interviews in that they provide the opportunity for open-ended response. While they lack the anonymity of interviews, they provide opportunities for participants to hear the thoughts of their colleagues and to build on one another's responses. They also are more cost-effective than individual interviews.

Data from both interviews and focus groups may be recorded (with the permission of participants) and transcribed. Software such as N-Vivo may then be used to identify emerging themes. While we use these techniques with major evaluations, often we ask interviewers to complete notes or meet with us and debrief as soon after the interview or focus group as possible.

CLASSROOM VISITATIONS

Although there are instances when in-depth lengthy observations are called for, in most cases we gather information through classroom visitations of three to five minutes. We train program evaluators to use the patterns of practice tool represented in Figure 10.8. (We also work with principals, teacher leaders, and district administrators to use this tool in their walk-throughs as a major component of instructional leadership.)

The patterns of practice tool provides a way to record multiple aspects of classroom practice including the following:

- Teacher focus and use of curriculum documents
- Teacher engagement
- Student engagement
- Research-based instructional strategies
- Instructional processes
- Assessment
- Questioning
- Use of technology

Trained observers can complete this form in two to three minutes. While data are usually collected for all categories on the form, analysis, discussion, and goal-setting at any given time may be more narrowly focused, on something like questioning, for example. The person collecting the patterns of practice enters the classroom and places a tally mark for each instance observed. Moving

Figure 10.7 Interview Protocol—Principals

Note: Queries reflect the key issues and areas to be discussed in interviews. Prompts may be used to stimulate discussion or to round out responses. Feel free to add prompts based on the tenor of the discussion but be aware of the time available and the *need to utilize all queries.*

Introduction

Thanks for taking the time to participate in this interview. All comments will be confidential and no individual will be cited or named in the report.

How is it determined what coaches work in your school?
What contextual factors promote or inhibit the work of coaches in your school? Content coaches: Instructional coaches:
Are activities being planned and conducted as you expected?
Is a solid management plan developed for the program?
What works well about the coaches program?
What gets in the way?

In what ways are the instruction coaches strategy and the content coaches strategy similar and different in purpose, delivery, and impact?
Which components of each program are most effective? Least effective? Need improvement?

Instructional Coaches
In general, how do instructional coaches spend time in your school?
Given multiple demands and limited time, how do instructional coaches determine which induction teachers to focus on, when, and for how long?
How do instructional coaches develop and maintain a collegial relationship with induction teachers? With mentors? With department chairs and team leaders? With you?
How do instructional coaches provide training and coaching on effective teaching strategies?
How do instructional coaches provide training and coaching in using data to improve instructional decision making?

Content Coaches
In general, how do content coaches spend their time in your school?
What has been the impact of coaches' own performance in the classroom?
What is the impact on coaches' decisions to remain in the profession?

Is there other information it is important for us to include in the report that results from the evaluation of the coaching programs?

Conclusion

[Thank participants for their time and insight. Provide the following e-mail address in case they have additional thoughts to share: CCRlearn@aol.com]

Figure 10.8 Patterns of Practice Data Sheet

School _____   Grade(s) _____   Date _____   Times _____

Cumulative Number of Classrooms Visited _____   Visitor _____

Subject(s): Is the S&S being used?									
	ELA	MATH	SCIENCE	SOCIAL STUDIES	OTHER	Teacher instructing	Teacher assessing	Teacher at desk	Teacher circulating	TA*
Adult Engagement	R W L S									S C W
Student Engagement	Noisy—Not paying attention	Quiet—Not paying attention	On task Quiet Noisy	Whole class	Responding to teacher questions	Independent work	Discussion, asking questions	Using tools, manipulatives, templates, graphic organizers	Working in centers	Reflection, self-assessment leading learning
High Yield Instructional Strategies (Marzano)	Objectives and feedback	Effort and recognition	Homework and practice	Questions, cues, advance organizers	Summarizing and note taking	Similarities and differences	Cooperative learning pairs and groups	Nonlinguistic representation	Hypotheses	Vocabulary
Instructional Process/ Feedback/ Assessment	Preassessment	Instruction and modeling	Guided practice	Independent practice	Selected response	Short answer	Products	Performances	Scoring guides	Accommodations or modifications
Questions	Lower order questions	higher-order questions	1–2 second wait time	3+ second wait time	Student responses factual	Student responses critical thinking	Technology** T S	Activating prior knowledge	Reading text	

*S = working with students; C = doing clerical work; W = watching

**T = teacher using technology; S = students using technology

Source: Center for Curriculum Renewal (www.curriculumrenewal.com). Used with permission.

to the next classroom, the process continues on the same sheet. No teacher names or classroom numbers are recorded, and data from no fewer than four classrooms are recorded on a form to assure teachers are not identified. Teams of teachers and the faculty as a whole can look at the patterns that emerge, discuss implications, and set desired targets for the next round of patterns-of-practice data collection. This process clarifies what practices are expected in a school and demonstrates the value placed on moving to routine use of the practices across classrooms throughout the school.

DOCUMENT REVIEW

In all program evaluations there is the need to review documents such as the curriculum guide, published and supplemental curriculum materials, lesson and unit plans, report cards, policies and procedures, schedules, and so forth. A major advantage of document review is that it is nonobtrusive—the documents are not influenced by the evaluation as people may be.

A major part of program evaluation is determining alignment: the degree to which the intended curriculum is aligned with practice. Document review is a major task in answering the alignment question.

Figure 10.9 provides an example of document review of an elementary social studies curriculum.

Figure 10.9　An Example of Document Review

Social Studies

Grades K–5

In 2001 and 2002, a group of teachers worked to develop a standards-based K–5 social studies curriculum based on New York State Learning Standards (hereafter, "the standards"). Susan Johnson, teacher on special assignment, facilitated the development of this curriculum.

The curriculum is based on the five standards: history of the United States and New York; world history; geography; economics, and civics, citizenship, and government.

It is organized by units consistent with the "expanding horizons" approach to social studies curriculum. A single unit has been assigned to each grade level as follows:

- Kindergarten—Self and others
- Grade 1—My family and other families, now and long ago
- Grade 2—My community and other United States communities
- Grade 3—Communities around the world—learning about people and places
- Local history and local government
- The United States, Canada, and Latin America

The curriculum at each grade level delineates concepts and themes. The document defines these terms as follows:

A *concept* is usually abstract—a product of the analysis and syntheses of facts and experiences rather than a definition—and constantly subject to change and expansion of meaning.

Thirteen key concepts are identified by New York for history; six for geography; five for economics; and nine for civics, citizenship, and government. These 33 concepts are specified for the social studies curriculum each year, kindergarten through Grade 12.

The *themes* are not explicitly defined in the curriculum. Examination of the document indicates that themes include such constructs as identity, change, empathy, and choice.

The curriculum is comprised of several sections, consistent across the K–5 curriculum. The *curriculum guide* is organized by unit and includes content standards, alignment with the standards (but not with key ideas or performance indicators). The curriculum guide also includes content understandings, concepts and themes, and a bank of key vocabulary terms.

The second section of the curriculum at each grade level is a *content activity planner*. This tool aligns recommended activities with the cognitive levels delineated in Bloom's taxonomy.

The curriculum also includes resources for instruction and assessment gleaned from New York State Test Prep, published materials, the Internet and other sources. These materials are not explicitly tied to either the curriculum guide or the content activity planner, nor are there explicit instructions for their use.

These locally developed resources are also with the New York State Core Curriculum. That document also is organized around units of study and includes content understandings and concepts and themes.

A BRIEF WORD ON ANALYSIS OF STUDENT PERFORMANCE DATA

While detailed discussion of analysis of student performance data is beyond the scope of this book, a discussion of the ways in which we analyze data is in order. We typically report statewide student performance data in terms of the percentage of students performing at each level of proficiency. We will disaggregate this data by subgroups (e.g., ethnicity, socioeconomic status, students with disabilities, English language learners). We will report the data longitudinally, following groups over time and cross-sectionally, to measure progress within a grade level.

Increasingly schools, districts, and states are embracing value-added analysis (Battelle for Kids, 2006). This process compares individual student performance to the student's own performance over time. The value-added process also measures the impact of the school on student growth over time by comparing student growth to a growth standard.

Typically the value-added metric is used in conjunction with, not instead of, student performance in relation to a standard and group achievement. Therefore, value-added schools have three related measures of accountability: student achievement as related to a standard, student growth as related to a growth standard, and school impact on student growth.

Value-added analysis is complex and is best approached through a major commitment to professional development and data analysis capacity at the district or state level. It is mentioned here because of its potential application to program evaluation in value-added settings.

In addition to reporting results on state assessments, we work with districts to develop common assessments, as described in Chapter 7.

Depending on the evaluation questions, we may add other local measures of student progress, such as writing portfolios or reading profiles. We also may report performance on external assessments such as SAT and ACT scores.

ALIGNING DATA SOURCES WITH EVALUATION QUESTIONS

There are several points you should bear in mind in selecting the specific data collection instruments you will use in your curriculum assessment.

1. Each instrument must be selected from existing ones or created. Be realistic in assessing the time and expertise available for creating new instruments.

2. Data collection and analysis is always harder and takes longer than anticipated. What can you realistically achieve in the time available?

3. Balance the need for multiple data sources with the possibility of overwhelming your respondents. This is a particular danger when the same teacher, parents, students, or others are involved in more than one type of data collection.

4. Gather all the data you need, and only the data you need.

Consider what data you will collect, who will be responsible for administering and collecting the data, who will be responsible for field testing (if locally developed), and dates for collection. You will want to field test your assessment with students other than those who will actually be assessed. This can be accomplished in several ways, such as field testing with students who complete the grade or course the following fall, field testing with students in a neighboring district, or field testing one year and implementing the next.

Use Worksheet 10.3 to match the program evaluation questions you created in Worksheet 10.2 with evaluation processes, replicating Figure 10.6 with your evaluation-based questions.

WORKSHEET 10.3 **Matching Program Evaluation Questions With Data Collection Methods**

Return to the program evaluation questions you developed. For each question, select the data collection processes you would use to inform your program evaluation.

Join a partner and explain your choices.
Provide feedback to your partner as to his or her choices.

Program Evaluation Questions	Methodology					
	Survey	Interview	Focus Groups/ Video Conf.	Classroom and School Visitations	Document Review	Data Analysis
Resources and conditions (input) questions						
Programs and practices questions						
Results questions						

FIELD TESTING

It is always best to field test each instrument first, particularly if it is one you have developed yourselves. The purpose of the field test is to ensure that the instrument provides the information required and to work out any kinks in the administration of the instrument. Field testing can also provide an excellent opportunity for training the data collectors.

Field testing is extremely important and is essential to a solid curriculum assessment. In the real world, however, it often does not occur. While there may be many reasons for this, lack of time and energy seem to be the primary culprits. Remember, however, that the considerable time and energy devoted to the development and implementation of the curriculum are not well served by a sloppy assessment process.

The field test should involve a small sample similar in nature to the target population, and it should occur under conditions as similar as possible to those that will exist during the actual data collection. A neighboring school or district often will provide a site for field testing.

CONDUCTING AND REPORTING THE PROGRAM EVALUATION

You have reviewed and practiced the processes of selecting program evaluation questions, basing them on your curriculum, and determining which of those questions should be included in the program evaluation. You have also practiced matching multiple data collection instruments to each question. Now you are ready to collect the information you need to answer each question, to analyze the data you collect, and to report results. This section provides a planning model to be used in making decisions regarding data collection, analysis, and reporting.

COLLECTING THE INFORMATION

Once the specific instruments have been selected and designed, the next step is to set up a process for collecting the information. Figure 10.10 shows a sample plan and timeline for data collection for an evaluation of a literacy-across-the-curriculum program. Use Worksheet 10.4 to formulate a plan and timeline for data collection.

TRAINING

Before using the instruments, it is important to train those who will administer them. This training may be very cursory, such as when a standardized test is to be administered, or it may be more complex, as when training observers and interviewers. In any case, it is essential that all gatherers of data be trained before the data gathering begins.

ANALYSIS OF THE DATA

Once the data has been collected, the next step is to arrange for its analysis. Data analysis can range from simple review and discussion to complex statistical manipulations. The data analysis process must be determined by the assessment questions and the nature of the assessment instruments used. If the questions require numeric representation to answer them, then statistics are needed. If not, a form of narrative or interpretive analysis will do the job.

Figure 10.10 Sample Program Evaluation Timeline

	Data Collection Event	Timing	By Whom	Of Whom
	Literacy Across the Curriculum (LAC) Evaluation			
1	Field test evaluation instruments	July	School Literacy Across the Curriculum Review Specialists (SLACRS)	Selected students, teachers, and parents
2	Student and parent climate survey	August	SLACRS	Selected students and parents
3	Student performance on state assessments	August	SLACRS	All students
4	Student demographic data	August	Measurement and Data Analysis Expert (MDAE)	State Department of Education or designated data person in district
5	School, district, and community characteristics	August	MDAE	Designated data person in each school and district
6	Administrator interviews	October	SLACRS	Principals and key central office staff
7	Teacher interviews	October	SLACRS	Selected staff
8	Professional development review and interview	October	District Reading Coordinator (DRC)	Professional developers in the program
9	Classroom observations	August through January	SLACRS	Randomly selected classrooms
10	Administrator survey	October and May	SLACRS	Selected administrators
11	Lesson plan review	September through February	SLACRS	Principals and key central office staff
12	Teacher survey	November	SLACRS	All participating and selected nonparticipating teachers
13	Observation of professional development workshops	August through December	SLACRS	Workshop participants
14	Development of findings and recommendations.	April	SLACRS	
15	Interim report to the district	May	SLACRS	
16	Presentation to the school board	May	SLACRS	
17	Final report	End of May	SLACRS	

It cannot be overemphasized that the tools used and the means of analysis chosen must be determined based on the assessment question and not the comfort level or preferences of the evaluators. Some people always gravitate more toward quantitative analysis (number crunching) or qualitative analysis without due consideration of the question at hand. Avoid these people in your data analysis process, and avoid being one yourself.

WORKSHEET 10.4 Program Evaluation Timeline Worksheet

	Data Collection Event	Timing	By Whom	Of Whom
1				
2				
3				
4				
5				
6				
7				
8				
9				
10				
11				
12				
13				
14				
15				
16				
17				

The following discussion frames the question of the type of analysis required for your program evaluation. There are three basic types of analysis commonly used in program evaluation processes.

The first type of analysis, *description,* is used when the assessment question requires a basic description of the sample or population. The three most common ways to describe something using statistics are in terms of central tendency, frequency, and variability.

- *Central tendency* describes the average behavior and is commonly expressed as mean, median, or mode.
- *Frequency* counts the number or percentage of persons in the sample behaving in a certain way.
- *Variability* tells how much the members of the sample or population differ from one another and is often expressed as standard deviation or variance.

Narrative description can be extremely rich and, for many assessment questions, far more appropriate than reduction to numbers. We typically use narrative description with open-ended survey questions, interviews, focus groups, and some aspects of observation and document review.

The second type of question deals with *relationship*—that is, the ways in which one variable relates to one or many others. Statistically, *correlation* is used to examine the relationship between two variables, and *regression* is used to describe the relationship between more than two variables. Relationships can also be explored and reported using narrative based on qualitative analysis methods such as those described above.

The last of the three most common types of analysis is *comparison,* which frequently requires comparing two or more groups to one another. In program evaluation, comparison often involves the analysis of variance of group performance on a given outcome. This can be done statistically by the analysis of variance and by similar methods for a variety of types of data.

Comparison can also be established using qualitative methods and reported narratively. The evaluator using qualitative methods scans the environment for relationships among persons or events in the assessment study. The evaluator develops working hypotheses about these relationships and constantly checks and refines these through ongoing observation of events and analysis of data. Very often a combination of quantitative and qualitative processes yields the richest data and the most useful results.

REPORTING RESULTS

Once the analysis of the data is complete, it is time to report the results of your curriculum assessment. Different groups will require different types of information. For example, parents may be very interested in student performance, but less interested in the design of the assessment. It is best to prepare a complete evaluation report, then prepare targeted reports for different audiences according to their needs. The complete report should include the following:

1. An introduction detailing the purposes of the assessment and a description of the curriculum area assessed

2. A list of the evaluation questions

3. A description of the design

4. A description of the data collection

5. Representation and discussion of the results

6. Findings, including the answer to each curriculum assessment question and unanticipated findings

7. Related recommendations

You should also prepare an executive summary of not more than two pages that provides a brief overview of the assessment and its major findings and recommendations. We also typically prepare a PowerPoint presentation of no more than six to eight slides for use in faculty, school board, and other public meetings.

Use Worksheet 10.5 to plan for the reporting of your curriculum assessment results.

Having completed the report, you need to decide where and when to disseminate it. Should it be distributed without comment, or are presentations necessary? Who should receive the results first? Are there aspects of the report that are for internal use only? Use Worksheet 10.6 to determine a schedule for sharing the results of the program evaluation.

Having completed the program evaluation, you are armed with data that can help you refine and revise your curriculum. The results will drive curriculum change, which will in turn lead to adjustments in implementation. Continual evaluation will ensure that the curriculum remains consistent with current research and best practice, and it will help to develop within the staff a disposition to active inquiry.

Program evaluation, while complex, is crucial to instructional improvement and is the force that maintains the curriculum as a vibrant, living document. It cannot be overlooked, dismissed, or ignored. Rather, it can become the substance of a truly professional learning community, one characterized by a focus on what is important for students to learn, how they best learn, and how their learning can best be demonstrated. For in the end, it is not the curriculum as it is written but rather the curriculum as it is truly learned that shapes people's lives.

WORKSHEET 10.5 Planning the Curriculum Evaluation Report

Section of Report	Responsibility	Completion Date
Introduction		
Evaluation questions		
Design		
Data collection		
Data analysis		
Findings		
Recommendations		
Executive summary		
PowerPoint		

WORKSHEET 10.6 Reporting the Program Evaluation Results

Constituency Group	Method of Reporting (written report, meeting, etc.)	Responsibility	Completion Date
Parents			
Community			
Faculty			
Administration			
School board			
Media			
Agencies (state/federal)			
Other			

References

Battelle for Kids. (2006). *Understanding and using value-added analysis.* Columbus, OH: Author.

Carr, J. F., & Harris, D. E. (2001). *Succeeding with standards: Linking curriculum, assessment, and action planning.* Alexandria, VA: Association for Supervision and Curriculum Development.

Carr, J. F., Harris, D. E., & Herman, N. (2005). *Creating dynamic schools through mentoring, coaching, and collaboration.* Alexandria, VA: Association for Supervision and Curriculum Development.

Eisner, E. (1985). *The educational imagination.* New York: Macmillan.

George, A. A., Hall, G. E., and Stiegelbauer, S. M. (2008). *Measuring implementation in schools: Stages of concern.* Austin, TX: Southwest Educational Development Laboratory.

Giroux, H., & Purpel, D. (Eds.). (1983). *The hidden curriculum and moral education.* Berkeley, CA: McCutchan.

Glickman, C. D., Gordon, S. P., & Ross-Gordon, J. (2007). *SuperVision and instructional leadership.* Boston: Allyn & Bacon.

Goodlad, J., & Associates. (1979). *Curriculum inquiry: The study of curriculum practice.* New York: McGraw-Hill.

Hall, G. E., Dirksen, D. J., & George, A. A. (2006). *Measuring implementation in schools: Levels of use.* Austin, TX: Southwest Educational Development Laboratory.

Hord, S. L., Rutherford, W. L., Huling-Austin, L., & Hall, G. E. (1987). *Taking charge of change.* Alexandria, VA: Association for Supervision and Curriculum Development.

Joyce, B., & Showers, B. (2002). *Student achievement through staff development* (3rd ed.). Alexandria, VA: Association for Supervision and Curriculum Development.

Loucks-Horsley, S. (1996). Professional development for science education: A critical and immediate challenge. In R. Bybee (Ed.), *National standards and the science curriculum: Challenges, opportunities, and recommendations* (pp. 83–95). Dubuque, IA: Kendall-Hunt.

Marzano, R. (2003). *What works in schools: translating research into action.* Alexandria, VA: Association for Supervision and Curriculum Development.

National Staff Development Council. (2001). *Standards for staff development (revised).* Oxford, OH: Author.

O'Neill, J. (2000). SMART goals, SMART schools. Educational Leadership. Quality Leadership by Design, LLC.

Reeves, D. B. (2005). *101 questions and answers about standards, assessment, and accountability.* Englewood, CO: Advanced Learning Press.

Rogers, P. (2007). *Using program theory and logic models in evaluation* [seminar]. Lewes, DE: The Evaluators Institute.

Rogers, V., & Stevenson, C. (1988). How do we know what kids are learning in school? *Educational Leadership, 45*(5), 68–75.

Roy, P. (2007). *A tool kit for quality professional development in Arkansas.* Oxford, OH: National Staff Development Council.

Schmoker, M. (2006). *Results now.* Alexandria, VA: Association for Supervision and Curriculum Development.

Studer, Q. (2008). *Results that last.* Hoboken, NJ: John Wiley.

Summers, L. (2008). *Setting SMART goals: an update of the classic guidelines.* Retrieved July 24, 2008, from http://www.greatleadershipbydan.com/2008/03/setting-smart-goals-update-of-classic.html.

Webb, N. (2002). *Depth-of-knowledge levels for four content areas.* Madison: University of Wisconsin–Madison, Wisconsin Center for Educational Research. Retrieved January 24, 2009 from http://facstaff.wcer.wisc.edu/normw/All%20content%20areas%20%20DOK%20levels%2032802.doc.

Index

Page references followed by *w* indicate a worksheet; followed by *fig* indicate an illustrated figure.

CORWIN

A SAGE Company